THE BOOK ON
VOLUNTEER
MANAGEMENT

Organize. Engage. Motivate.

Written by Eric Burger
Edited by Gabrielle Long
Produced by VolunteerHub

CONTENTS

ACKNOWLEDGEMENT

Thank you to all the people on our team who have worked together over the years to assemble the knowledge in this book, as well as our nonprofit customers who've contributed many ideas and suggestions along the way. I'd especially like to thank Eric, for the many hours he spent organizing and writing the text, and Gabrielle, for her tireless editing, formatting, and project oversight.

Dr. Michael Carr
CEO & Founder
Carr Engineering, Inc. (creators of VolunteerHub)

THE HISTORY OF VOLUNTEERISM IN AMERICA

An action ingrained in the human spirit.

*"Volunteering is at the very core of being a human.
No one has made it through life without someone else's help."*

—*Heather French Henry*

Volunteerism has made a difference in the lives of others for many years. The first known examples of volunteerism date back to the early 18th century. The act of volunteering probably goes back much farther than that, as the process of helping people is ingrained in the human spirit. In 1736, Benjamin Franklin founded the first volunteer-run firehouse, Union Fire Company, in Philadelphia, PA.[1] Franklin believed that the fire and rescue process needed to be improved, that training should be provided and that volunteers could make an impact on the system as a whole. Franklin wrote about the need for better firefighting processes in his publication, the Pennsylvania Gazette, before forming the volunteer-run firehouse on December 7, 1736.[2]

Union Fire Company utilized 30 volunteers at a time to achieve their mission of saving lives in Philadelphia.[3] All of the equipment used by the Union Fire Company was also provided by the volunteers that staffed it. Volunteers agreed to provide leather buckets and stout linen bags as a part of their commitment to the cause. Volunteers at the Union Fire Company also agreed to meet up to eight times a year and pay a fee that could be used to fund equipment and other expenses needed by the firehouse. Benjamin Franklin and the Union Fire Company volunteer initiative set the stage for fire safety practices, training, and firehouse volunteer programs of the future. Today, over 70% of firefighters in the United States are volunteers according to a National Fire Protection Association (NFPA) report.[4]

THE REVOLUTIONARY WAR

The American Revolutionary War (April 1775 – September 3, 1783) also demanded volunteerism in the North American colonies. The war began due to tensions between American colonies and the British government. The British government demanded that American colonies pay a large percentage of debt caused by the French and Indian war. The British government also began to tax Americans at what was considered an unfair rate. These actions sparked a war. War-time created a need for equipment and support from families on the mainland. North America boycotted British products and collected money to provide funds for war-time support and equipment in an initiative that showed patriotism during a time of conflict.

Volunteers also stepped up to the frontline and provided their service in battle. These volunteer soldiers were called "Minutemen," as they were often needed with little to no notice. Minutemen were independently formed militia groups who fought for America's freedom. Most men serving as Minutemen were self-trained in the act of combat and did not have any prior experience in war. Minutemen were typically young, reliable, and physically strong. It is estimated that 25% of the militia served as Minutemen during the Revolutionary War. Therefore, with the help of volunteerism, the

Continental Army, led by George Washington, defeated the armies of the British empire in 1783.

THE GREAT AWAKENING

The 19th century saw some big changes in the act of volunteerism. Volunteerism became a more organized initiative primarily formed through religious organizations. Notably, America saw the second Great Awakening, a movement brought to fruition in the 1790s that gained momentum in the 1830s. The second Great Awakening was a religious revival with an emphasis on evangelism, and it inspired people to get involved in volunteerism in an effort to make a difference in the world. The calling, geared towards young people, requested involvement through religious organizations with a primary mission of helping the homeless and creating other relief programs across the United States. The Great Awakening helped to create networks of people and charitable organizations interested in fighting specific causes. Several nonprofit organizations leaving a large footprint today were born from the Great Awakening movement that lasted through the remainder of the 19th century.[5]

The Young Men's Christian Association (YMCA), the oldest and largest charity for youths, is one such nonprofit that took root as a by-product of the Great Awakening movement. The organization was founded on June 6, 1844, in London, England, by George Williams. Williams, a department store worker, saw a need to provide resources to young men migrating to the city from rural areas. The original goal of the YMCA was to provide fellowship, prayer, bible study, and support to individuals residing on the overcrowded and dangerous city streets of England. The organization quickly gained momentum and soon had a presence in North America in 1851. Today, there are 2,700 YMCA locations nationwide that employ 20,000 full-time staff members and 600,000 volunteers.[6]

The American Red Cross was also formed during the Great Awakening period. The organization was founded in 1881 by Clarissa Harlowe Barton. Before establishing the American Red Cross, Barton provided services and supplies to soldiers fighting in the Civil War, often risking her life to assist these soldiers on the front line. Barton formed the Red Cross 16 years after the war in an effort to provide support to people in distress. The American Red Cross received their first congressional charter in the year 1900 and to this day continues to provide services to the armed forces and victims of disasters around the world.[7] Today, The American Red Cross employs 35,000 people and is supported by 500,000 volunteers.

Another well-known organization that was born during the Great Awakening period is United Way. United Way was founded in Denver, CO, in 1887 by Frances Wisebart Jacobs, Rev. Myron W. Reed, Msgr. William J. O'Ryan, Dean H. Martyn Hart, and Rabbi William S. Friedman. The organization's goal was to support local charities through fundraising, coordinating relief services, referring clients to network agencies, and providing emergency assistance grants.[8] The United Way raised over $20,000 dollars, a considerable amount at the time, in its first year. Since its inception, United Way has utilized 2.8 million volunteers to realize their mission.

WORLD WAR I

The act of volunteerism evolved significantly during the 20th century in America. Believe it or not, the term "nonprofit" was not widely accepted until 1915. In the early 1900s, the use of volunteers started to become more mainstream than ever before. Many of the organizations employing volunteers were formed to support wartime efforts during World War I. Following the sinking of four U.S. merchant ships by a German cruiser, the United States declared war against Germany on April 2, 1917, and prepared to send troops to France to begin training for war. The first U.S. troops arrived in France on June 26, 1917, three years after the war had begun.[9]

The United States was involved in World War I for about 7 months, during which 116,000 Americans were killed and much more were injured. On November 11, 1918, Germany finally surrendered, and all nations agreed to stop fighting and formally end the war on June 28, 1919, with the signing of the Treaty of Versailles.

According to the Red Cross, approximately 90,000 volunteers worked at home and abroad during World War I.[10] These volunteers provided a number of services in the wartime effort, some of which included voluntary aid detachments, medical training, special services, general services, air raid duty, and transportation services. As a result, an estimated 18,000 new charities were established during the war.[11] Many of these organizations focused on providing troops with clothing, medical services, food, post-war remembrance, and support. Many of the soldiers fighting in battle were also volunteers. In Great Britain alone, 2,675,149 men volunteered.[12]

THE GREAT DEPRESSION: A NEED FOR VOLUNTEERISM

The period between World War I and World War II was another time in America's history featuring a strong calling for the support of volunteerism: the Great Depression. The Great Depression was the worst economic downturn in history and began when the stock market crashed in October of 1929 after traders sold 12.9 million shares of stock in a single day, which became known as "Black Thursday."[13] Many families lost everything during the Great Depression and were forced to sell their businesses and drain their savings. Between 1929 and 1932, 25% of the national workforce had become unemployed, a rate that jumped nearly 22% from the national average of 3% in the years before. Income levels also dropped an average of 42% for individuals who were still employed. High unemployment rates and sharp drops in income sparked a huge increase in the number of homeless and nearly homeless families around the world. No one was prepared for the financial devastation caused on Black Thursday and the ten years of rebuilding that would follow.

President Herbert Hoover believed that the support of people would be the saving grace for the sour economic times, and only with their support would the economy prevail. And he was right; the Great Depression saw one of the first large-scale efforts to coordinate volunteerism for a specific need. The people in the United States and around the world were suffering and needed support, and volunteers stepped into action by providing shelter, running soup kitchens, operating breadlines, and even providing some families with work. Many nonprofit groups came together to provide the basic necessities of life.

Two years after President Franklin Roosevelt took office in 1933, he signed the "New Deal," which created 42 agencies with the goal of developing jobs, creating unionization, and providing individuals with unemployment insurance.

The Great Depression ended in 1939, just before the commencement of World War II.

THE SECOND WORLD WAR

World War II began on September 1, 1939, when Nazi Germany attacked Poland, and the United States began their involvement following the bombing of Pearl Harbor on December 7, 1941, resulting in the deaths of 2,408 Americans. World War II quickly became the deadliest military conflict in history. It is estimated that, by the time the war ended on September 2, 1945, over 70,000,000 people worldwide were killed.[14] With conflict, devastation, and need came a calling for volunteerism.

Volunteers had a large impact on the war, both on the battlefield and from the homefront. Volunteers at home contributed by rationing consumer goods, recycling materials, buying war bonds, and working in war industries. The war brought people on the homeland together in an effort to protect freedom and their general way of life. Many individuals also volunteered their time to serve on the battlefield, including women for the first time. More than 11,000 women enlisted in the Navy by the end of the second World War.

With injured soldiers also came the need for medical and nursing volunteers to assist near the frontline of combat. The Red Cross was actively involved during World War II and is responsible for creating the first nationwide civilian blood program, a program that still benefits many people today.

VOLUNTEERISM CONTINUES TO EVOLVE

Post-World War II, volunteerism in America has continued to grow and become a widely accepted way for people to become involved in the greater good. America itself was changing as well. The Civil Rights Movement called for us to come together as a nation and fight for equality. The War in Vietnam asked for civilian support in the way of volunteerism. In the late 20th century, the government began to provide nonprofit organizations with more support. The Tax Reform Act was passed in 1969 to allow organizations that met specific guidelines to declare themselves a "private foundation," which offered many benefits such as tax exemptions to organizations in the nonprofit space.

The history of volunteerism provided a foundation that allowed the act of volunteering to evolve into what it means today: an indispensable resource for the betterment of communities worldwide.

VOLUNTEERISM IN THE 21ST CENTURY

Making the world a better place, one volunteer at a time.

"Never doubt that a small group of thoughtful, committed citizens can change the world; indeed, it's the only thing that ever has."

—Margaret Mead

The history of volunteerism has paved the way for how we approach the action today. The process and reach of nonprofits worldwide have changed a lot over the past decades, but the end goal of fighting for worthwhile causes remains the same. In today's technological world we now have the power to measure and understand the impact that volunteerism makes around us, an ability that was only dreamed about until the 21st century. We also have the ability to understand who volunteers are and what compels them to provide organizations with their time and often their financial resources. We will explore the evolution of the average volunteer in a later chapter, but we first need to discuss what volunteerism looks like in the 21st century, what common causes nonprofits are addressing, what challenges nonprofits face today, and what impact volunteerism is making around the world.

As of 2017, there are over 1.4 million tax-exempt nonprofit organizations in the United States alone and over 62 million volunteers providing their time to those organizations. Nonprofit employees today make up about 10% of the American workforce, comprising the third largest growing sector according to an independent study.[15] Volunteerism has become much more widely accepted today than in generations before. Until now, the act of volunteering was often thought of as an act only performed by the wealthy. Today, 25% of the adult population donates their energy in a selfless effort to make a difference.

NONPROFIT LANDSCAPE OF THE 21ST CENTURY

According to an article published by Shorter University, there are 5 types of nonprofit organizations today. These organizations can be classified as public charities, foundations, social advocacy groups, professional trade organizations, and fraternal societies. The causes these types of organizations stand behind range from community support, children and youth, education, health and medicine, advocacy, human rights, animal rights, homelessness, housing and much more. The options for where volunteers provide their time today and what causes they support is immense.

The most common charities in the 21st century are public charities, according to BoardSource. Public charities receive their funding from government, individuals, corporations, and foundation sources. A few examples of public charities include hospitals, museums, and libraries. These organizations provide services for the betterment of the community they serve. The 21st century has also seen a rise in the number of small nonprofits. A survey by the Council of Nonprofits found that close to 30% of nonprofits have a budget of less than $100,000.[16] These organizations are often started by people who have previously been affected by the issue on which they're trying to make an impact.

Nonprofits both large and small are making a quantifiable difference in the world, such as City Rescue Mission, which in 2016 provided more than 350,000 meals and 130,000 nights of shelter. Metropolitan Ministries developed a self-sufficiency program to create long-term success and stability for the homeless and near homeless in and around Florida. Habitat for Humanity builds and repairs homes for people in need. Nonprofits nationwide are taking steps and making goals to solve real-world issues. The list of nonprofits making a substantial difference could go on and on. A good thing for the world in which we live.

Check out the case studies on volunteerhub.com that demonstrate the differences organizations are making in the community.

TRAGEDY, DISASTERS, AND WAR-TIME RELIEF EFFORTS OF THE 2000'S

As with earlier generations, the 21st century has presented challenges and tragedies that nations have had to overcome. During these trying times, nonprofits and their volunteers have stepped up to the calling to provide support to those affected.

One such tragedy that shook the world took place in the United States on Tuesday, September 11, 2001. On that tragic day, terrorists attacked the nation by commandeering four airplanes in mid-flight. Two of the aircraft were flown directly into the World Trade Center in New York City, another into the Pentagon, and the fourth crashed in Shanksville, PA. Almost 3,000 people lost their lives from this horrific attack on their home soil. These attacks on the United States, known by most today as 9/11, sparked thousands to come to the aid of others as volunteers. Volunteer police officers, fireman, emergency response units, medical personnel and many others in various roles came to the aid of victims after the attack. Volunteers assisted injured victims, cleared debris, evacuated large groups, and provided general support.

Other volunteers, like those with the New York City Fire Department, risked their own lives to reach those who were stranded at the tops of the World Trade Center towers. These brave men and woman did not know if they would make it back out of the burning buildings but believed enough in the cause to take that chance. Many nonprofit agencies also assisted in the organized relief effort, including The Red Cross and the Mayor's Volunteer Action Center. America may never truly heal from the devastation that was caused on September 11, 2001, but the events did demonstrate the compassion that many of its citizens have for others in need of help.

The 21st century has also proven to be a time in which volunteers came together worldwide to aid others in natural disasters. In the past two decades, a number of natural disasters, including hurricanes like Katrina and Irma, took the lives of over 2,200 people in the United States. In 1996, Canada endured the Saguenay flood, which destroyed 800 homes and took the lives of ten people, in addition to numerous floods in the decade that followed. Volunteers and support agencies played a key role in providing services to help recover after these natural disasters, yet the future held even more devastation that would show the true value and urgency of volunteerism across the globe.

There have been many disasters that called for the assistance of world-wide volunteerism. In 2010, Haiti was hit by one of the biggest earthquakes of all time claiming the lives of over 200,000 people. The aftermath of the disaster required an international relief operation. The United States alone sent thousands of military troops and volunteers to deliver supplies, provide search and rescue services, and help maintain order.[17] World-wide governments and individuals have donated billions of dollars to help Haiti recover since the disaster. The recovery effort is still taking place today.

Another disaster requiring global volunteerism in the 21st Century was the Tohoku earthquake and Tsunami that hit the east coast of Japan in 2011. The earthquake killed at least 15,000, destroyed over 120,000 buildings, and has been classified as the 4th most powerful earthquake in the world.[18] Nations from across the globe came together to assist Japan's recovery, providing yet another example of how great people come together regardless of background or nationality to lend support to others in need on a global scale.

Natural disasters are just one of the many use cases for volunteers around the world. As with previous generations, volunteers of the 21st century have also been used in war-time aid. The War in Iraq, for instance, lasted over eight years, during which volunteers from the United States and abroad assisted by donating financial resources, food, and other resources to soldiers and veterans in need of aid. Regardless of cause, the problems of our time make it easy to see that the efforts of nonprofits and their volunteers are the glue that holds our world together in times of need.

NONPROFIT HURDLES OF THE 21ST CENTURY

In order to understand how nonprofits are different today than ever before it is important to look at some of the hurdles that organizations must overcome to be successful. The way that nonprofits operate today is much different than they did in previous generations. Nonprofit organizations today operate much like for-profit organizations. Most have internal staff, leadership teams, and many have relationships with large corporate organizations who help fund their efforts. Like organizations in the for-profit industry nonprofits also have hurdles that they have to overcome to improve their operations and efficiency.

The first of the four most common issues that nonprofits struggle with today is sustainability, or the ability to maintain resources and fulfill long-term goals. To be sustainable, a nonprofit organization needs to make decisions that align with its mission and values. There are several additional steps that nonprofits can take to be sustainable in the 21st century, including:

- Taking the time to create a mission and vision statement that are sincere and align with organizational goals.
- Creating consistent messaging across all mediums.

- Understanding the nonprofit's prospects and supporters fully and taking them into consideration when making organizational decisions.
- Focusing efforts on creating strategic partnerships that enhance outreach ability.
- Analyzing and identifying problem areas that could affect the organization both short-term and long-term.

The second most common struggle for nonprofits in the 21st century is effectively engaging volunteers. Engagement means everything for volunteer and donor prospects of the 21st century. The web is an important component of engagement that was not readily available for generations before. Today, the average donor retention rates for offline-only donors is 29%, and online-only donors average a 21% retention rate as of 2017.[19] A study by Blackbaud also found that 3 out of every 4 new donors leave and never look back.[20] These are troubling numbers in the nonprofit space. Raising these averages just a few percentage points can mean more reach and financial resources for organizations to use toward fulfilling their missions.

Nonprofits can engage donors in a variety of strategic ways. A few of the most successful strategies for donor engagement include:

- Investing in and providing volunteers with an in-depth, quality training program.
- Taking the time to get to know volunteers personally and providing opportunities that align with a specific volunteer's skillset and values.
- Engaging volunteers by providing rewards and recognition for their service.
- Incorporating gamification into engagement strategy.
- Effectively communicating with volunteers across multiple communication streams.

Third, many nonprofits today struggle to find the funding necessary to fulfill their mission. The rise in nonprofit organizations of the 21st century makes competition fierce, as donors have a lot of options when choosing where to give. Most nonprofits also receive funding from multiple sources, requiring a variety of strategies for attracting donors and, as a result, often producing a cumbersome process. Many nonprofits fail to secure funding because they lack the ability to:

- Retain their existing donors.
- Build trust with current donor base and/or prospects.
- Convert volunteers to donors.
- Identify and harness a relationship with corporate donors.
- Use cost-effective fundraising avenues.
- Capture, understand, and leverage data about their donors.

Successful nonprofits know how to engage and retain their donor base, tell the right stories to the right people, identify and cultivate strategic partnerships, and take advantage of cost-effective fundraising streams.

The fourth challenge for 21st-century nonprofits is creating a strategic and effective succession plan. Succession planning is the process of identifying and developing new leaders who will replace existing leaders in the future. In other words, how would your organization's volunteer and donor programs function if any member of your staff were to suddenly leave? Not having a succession plan in place can lead to unwarranted process changes, a blurred vision, inconsistent experience for supporters and the potential of other nonprofit management issues. Harvard Business Review published four great tips when creating a succession plan:[21]

- Focus your effort on succession development and not planning.
- Measure your outcomes and let them dictate your process.
- Develop a plan based on simplicity.
- Be realistic about your succession plan expectations.

Creating a nonprofit that is successful in fulling its mission for the long-term can be very challenging in today's busy nonprofit sector. Organizations need to stand out from the crowd, create compelling messaging, attract donors and volunteers, be sustainable, create a process, and streamline their efficiencies. With the right planning and execution, it is possible to create a successful nonprofit that makes a large-scale difference in the community.

HOW VOLUNTEERISM HAS CHANGED IN THE 21ST CENTURY

In order to tap into new skillsets while also combatting some of the fundraising issues nonprofits typically, many nonprofits today are looking for traditional volunteers and individuals to fill skill-based opportunities. There are even some organizations that are 100% volunteer-operated. Skill-based volunteerism, a relatively new concept, leverages the talents of individuals to strengthen a nonprofit's infrastructure and capacities. Skill-based opportunities range in function but often include departments such as administrative, operations, marketing, management, financial, IT, legal and other professional services. A recent study found that skill-based volunteerism is valued 500% more than traditional volunteering.[22] The same study determined that 92% of nonprofits in the United States do not have enough pro-bono support.

These statistics are not meant to dilute or devalue the traditional volunteer's contributions to an organizations mission; rather, they demonstrate that the need for volunteerism as a whole is evolving to include new avenues for providing support to a cause. Nonprofits still would not be able to fulfill their missions without traditional volunteers providing their time. In fact, the value of the traditional volunteer is also on the rise: As of 2017, a volunteer hour is valued at $24.14, a value that's up 2.5% compared with 2016 and is expected to continue to grow.[23] Volunteerism as a whole is estimated to surpass $171 billion for 2017.

Technology has also changed the way volunteers sign up for opportunities. Some volunteers have the ability to provide their support to organizations from home, often filling professional roles, fundraising capacities and more. Technology is making it easier than ever for nonprofits to communicate, fill, and manage their opportunities. Volunteer management software is freeing up nonprofits' time to focus on other aspects of the organization, such as engagement and retention.

Finally, the average volunteer has changed substantially over the years. As part of that change, a widening age range for volunteerism has led to challenges when appealing to and recruiting younger generations of volunteers.

Here are a few demographical statistics to consider:[24]

- Individuals between the ages of 35 and 54 are most likely to volunteer their time.
- Women are more likely to volunteer their time than men.
- Volunteer rates are the lowest for individuals between the ages of 20 and 24.
- Married individuals are 10% more likely to volunteer than those who are not married.
- Individuals with higher education levels are more likely to volunteers than those without.
- Most volunteers (approximately 72%) provide support to one or two organizations only.

The need for volunteers, both skill-based and traditional, as well as the value of volunteerism itself have increased considerably over the years. As a result, the methods organizations use to find, recruit, engage, and manage volunteers has changed considerably over the years. The next step, then, is to understand how and why those methods have evolved, beginning with identifying how to motivate your organization's supporters.

CHANGES TO VOLUNTEERISM AND VOLUNTEER MOTIVATIONS

"Volunteers don't get paid, not because they're worthless, but because they're priceless."

—Sherry Anderson

Nonprofits' ability to affect the greater good has changed and adapted over the years. Technology continues to allow nonprofits to touch the lives of more people than ever before. Organizational and process changes are not the only adapting variable affecting nonprofit's around the world, however. Volunteers, the foundation of the sector, are also changing and adapting to the times. Today, if a nonprofit wants to reach and retain volunteers, it understanding what motivates them to give, how to engage supporters, and what volunteers today expect in return for their commitment is essential.

Before diving into what motivates volunteers today, let's look at a few volunteer statistics to better understand the impact of volunteerism today. In the United States for the year 2017 alone:

- 62.6 million citizens volunteered their time
- Volunteers committed a total of 7.8 billion hours
- Volunteerism was worth over 184 billion dollars

This data showcases the important role volunteerism plays in providing nonprofits with the resources they need to achieve their goals. What, then, is the motivation behind this incredible value? in other words, what motivates volunteers to provide their time to a cause, how can your nonprofit leverage these motivations, and how can your organization develop strategic processes to continue to drive new supporters and retain existing ones based on these behaviors and trends?

VOLUNTEER MOTIVATIONS

Volunteers today donate their time for a plethora of reasons. Nonprofits that can identify these reasons and create messaging around them are typically more successful at attracting new supporters. Nonprofits that do not fully understand their volunteers and their motivations for providing their time can lack the ability to reach their target audience and fill opportunities with the right volunteer prospect.

Did you know that, according to an Independent Sector study, 71% of people asked to volunteer actually do? Asking prospects to volunteer is one of the top reasons volunteers commit their time and can actually be accomplished in a variety of ways, such as through a referral from other organization supporters or through marketing efforts. One of the most successful ways to reach potential volunteer candidates is to improve your organization's relationship with existing volunteers. Your volunteer-base has access to their own personal connections and most likely would be happy to provide referrals if your nonprofit delivers a valuable experience in exchange for their time. Referrals can be one of the most valuable recruitment streams for your organization, as trust is higher within a prospect's personal network.

The second most common motivation for volunteerism is that a supporter has a personal connection with a nonprofit's cause and/or mission. These types of volunteers can often be your organization's most valuable asset because they want to see your nonprofit reach its goals. Organizations can appeal to this type of motivation by telling captivating stories. Effective and relatable storytelling can elicit emotions that a potential prospect has dealt with personally. Your nonprofit should also consider reaching out to past clients about opportunities to volunteer. Chances are they will want to pay it forward in the form of volunteerism.

Third, a lot of volunteers are motivated by the desire to learn new skills that can benefit them in their own personal life and work life. Providing prospects with career development opportunities is a great way to entice them to volunteer. Did you know that 41% of hiring managers considered volunteer experience to be as valuable as paid work experience?[25] There are many volunteer prospects that consider volunteer work as a positive step toward their desired career field. Providing volunteers with career development opportunities allows supporters to:

- Engage in valuable networking opportunities.
- Retain new skills and sharpen existing ones.
- Practice deploying their skills in a low-risk environment.
- Explore new career paths.
- Brush up on leadership skills.

The fourth most common reason that people volunteer today is that volunteerism has been shown to offer participants health benefits. Obviously, volunteerism is a selfless activity that touches the lives of others every day, but the action can also improve the lives of those who serve. According to United Health Group, 96% of volunteers claim that the action has provided them not only with a sense of enrichment and purpose in life, but also the following health benefits:[26]

- A study found that 96% of survey participants feel happier after volunteering.[27] In addition, volunteerism decreases loneliness by providing participants with socialization opportunities.
- According to that same study, 73% of surveyed volunteers reported a reduction in stress after their volunteer experience.
- Volunteering has been shown to combat and reduce Alzheimer's disease.
- Volunteering can provide participants with physical health benefits.

Fifth, and one of the most common motivations for volunteerism, is a sense of purpose. Many volunteers are compelled to provide their time in exchange for the opportunity to fulfill a desire to make the world a better place for themselves and others. Their commitment to causes all over the world is most certainly making a substantial difference. Did you know that the nonprofit sector contributes more than $878 billion dollars a year to the economy?[28] The nonprofit industry is also stimulating the economy through job creation. According to the Bureau of Labor Statistics, the nonprofit sector employs over 10% of the American workforce. These statistics do not even begin to demonstrate the difference that nonprofits around the world are making on the communities they serve and the people directly impacted by their cause. Volunteering gives people the opportunity to commit their time to address issues they feel strongly about.

Sixth, some individuals volunteer because they are required to do so. This requirement may be for school, work, extra-curricular activities or potentially to fill a court-ordered obligation. A 2012 study found that 31% of teens volunteer because it is required, and another 63% of teens volunteer with no outside requirement.[29] Some extra-curricular activities also have service requirements such as Boy Scout and Girl Scout programs as well as various youth groups. For example, Eagle Scout prospects are required to fulfill at least 18 hours of service to increase their ranks. Finally, some individuals are required by the court to engage in volunteer service. Court-ordered community service is becoming a common alternative to jail time and fines and allows an individual to fulfill their requirement with the courts and do good at the same time.

Last but not least, some volunteers are motivated to commit their time in exchange for a reward or recognition. The importance of thanking volunteers and making the volunteer experience fun and engaging has never been so important as it is today. Volunteers have more options than ever as to where they provide their time, and they expect to be provided value in exchange for their commitment to a cause.

MOTIVATION-LEAD RECRUITMENT STRATEGIES

There are many reasons why volunteers are willing to donate their time. Understanding your volunteers' motivations and leveraging them to improve your recruitment strategies is one of the most important steps your organization can take to find the right talent for a specific role. Understanding those motivations can also help your organization become data-driven and implement more effective outreach strategies based on volunteer behavior. Therefore, it's important to understand how to appeal to each of the top motivation types.

Volunteers that are motivated by being asked to participate are the easiest group to reach. Nurture your organization's existing volunteer-base and use current supporters as referral sources. Your organization also should also focus on creating a list of prospects and composing messaging to those prospects that compels individuals to consider learning more about upcoming opportunities. Prospects that fit into this category are waiting for your nonprofit to reach out with a compelling ask. Engage these types of prospects with details regarding the impact that your organization can make with their help. Ask prospects to join your cause via both inbound marketing strategies, such as blogs, social media, and search engine optimization, as well as outbound marketing strategies, such as email, telemarketing, press releases, and direct mail.

An effective storytelling strategy is the best method to reach prospects that are motivated by your nonprofit's mission and cause. Creating enticing stories can create buzz and increase the number of prospects interested in committing their time. Here are a few ways to tell better stories about your organization's cause, mission, values, and goals:

- Let prospects visualize your mission and make it compelling by including stories that demonstrate the impact your organization has made on the community.
- Provide prospects with examples and outcomes of how your organization is making an impact today and what you can achieve tomorrow.
- Incorporate an emotional trigger into your storytelling campaigns.
- Provide your prospects with the insights, next steps, and details they need to make a decision. Volunteers are more likely to become engaged when provided next steps to become involved.
- Leverage your organizational data to gauge how prospects prefer to consume storytelling content. Do they prefer short blog articles, or do they tend to engage more with email blasts?
- Choose storytelling content your prospects can relate to so they can see themselves as an asset as well as feel a personal connection to your purpose.
- Ensure the information shared with prospects is accurate and authentic.

Volunteers seeking career development opportunities in exchange for their time can benefit from an abundance of opportunities, including networking and learning new skills. Your nonprofit can create a career development program that appeals to prospects and fills skill-based opportunities at the same time. Did you know that 92% of nonprofits say they need more skill-based, pro bono support?[30] A recruitment strategy based on career development may fill that void for your organization. Here are a few ways to appeal to volunteers looking for career development opportunities:

- Focus part of your plan on mentorship and offer volunteers the opportunity to learn from others who possess their desired skill set.

- Allow your volunteers to be leaders and explore opportunities outside their comfort zone.
- Encourage volunteers to network and build their personal connection list.
- Provide volunteers with real-world challenges to allow them to grow professionally.
- Advertise your organization's career development opportunities on job boards.
- Optimize your career development program based on feedback from supporters. This will help make your program more appealing.

Another motivation type that we discussed previously is the desire to reap the health benefits that volunteerism has to offer. The best way to recruit for this type of motivation is to remind the community that these health benefits exist. Your organization should consider incorporating a wellness plan into your volunteer program to leverage the health benefits even further. Communicating the health benefits of volunteerism conveys your organization's interest in the wellbeing of both your supporters and the community.

If your organization utilizes volunteers who are required to participate in a community service program, your nonprofit will want to prepare for and recruit volunteers from this category effectively and carefully. Reach out to your local schools, government agencies and court systems to build strong relationships with officials in the community.

Effectively recruiting volunteers starts by understanding what truly motivates them to give their time. Whether volunteers are fulfilling a requirement or a personal desire to volunteer, or perhaps are simply being asked to give back to the community, your organization should have a toolset of engagement strategies at the ready for any type of volunteer.

VOLUNTEER MANAGEMENT BEST PRACTICES

"Life's most persistent and urgent question is, what are you doing for others?"

—*Martin Luther King, Jr.*

A s we discussed in the previous chapter, volunteer motivations have evolved over time. Volunteers are looking to receive value in return for the commitment that they provide to your organization, and this value can come in the form of both internal and external gains. Creating a volunteer program that appeals to supporters is one of the best ways to sustain your organization long-term and make a bigger impact in the community that your nonprofit serves. Keeping in mind that a volunteer hour is worth over $23 USD and continues to grow, each year nonprofits are finding new ways to utilize volunteerism to fill a variety of roles that make a big impact on their bottom lines. Taking the time to create an effective volunteer program is worth the effort and will pay off in dividends down the road.

In this chapter, we will define volunteer management and discuss several best practices for developing and implementing a successful program that fulfills your nonprofit's needs. We will also explore volunteer management software and how a technology solution can improve your nonprofit's visibility into its volunteer program, streamline processes, recruit talent and make the act of volunteering more fun for your supporters.

WHAT IS VOLUNTEER MANAGEMENT?

Volunteer management can best be defined as a strategic process. The ultimate goal of the process should be determined based on the overarching mission, values, and goals of each unique nonprofit. Determining what your organization hopes to gain from managing your volunteer-base is the best place to start in defining what volunteer management means to you. A few of the most common volunteer management goals are to motivate, lead, supervise, and understand an organization's volunteer-base. Effective volunteer management can help to create a strategic path for organizations to recruit and retain supporters, monitor activity, and leverage data trends for the betterment of their program. Implementing a strategic volunteer management plan can help your organization become a data-driven nonprofit that allows volunteer behavior to dictate program decision-making.

DEVELOPING A VOLUNTEER MANAGEMENT PLAN

How your organization implements and manages volunteers is dependent upon the goals and mission you are trying to reach. That being said, there are several best practices that successful volunteer management programs typically focus around. On the following pages, we will discuss three best practices that your organization should incorporate into your volunteer management strategy, each of which can help your nonprofit determine which volunteer metrics should be measured and how your organization can use that data to determine success and program pitfalls.

LAY THE PROGRAM FOUNDATION

As with every strategic process that your nonprofit implements, laying the foundation for your volunteer management program is the best place to start. It is key that leadership within your organization is on-board with a better volunteer management process from the start and understands what problems a strategic process will solve. In this stage, your organization should determine expectations and rules for your volunteer management strategy that will create internal transparency for the program. A great way to begin laying the framework for your volunteer management program as well as to communicate purpose with stakeholders is by creating a vision. Your volunteer management vision should answer a few key questions:

- How many volunteers will it take to reach your desired outcomes? How will volunteer management assist in this process?
- What roles do you want volunteers to fill in order to push your nonprofit forward and drive your organization closer to its mission. How will volunteer management help in identifying and filling these opportunities?
- What additional opportunities and roles could your organization create with a larger volunteer pool?
- What will your volunteer program offer volunteers in exchange for their commitment? Where does volunteer management come in?
- How will a volunteer management program create sustainability for your organization in the future?

CREATE A REALISTIC TIMELINE

Once your organization has determined your volunteer management vision, the next step is to create a timeline and implementation plan. Remember that creating a strategic volunteer management plan takes time;

patience is key, as you do not want to miss any important variables that could change the overall scope and goals of the program. Here are a few steps that your organization should take build an implementation timeline for your volunteer management project:

- Identify who in your organization will be involved in creating and implementing the program. Make a plan for each contributor's role and the goals they are responsible for achieving.
- Make your program creation goals realistic in relation to the time your organization is able to designate toward it.
- Focus on accomplishing easy tasks first. Completing these tasks will help your organization see progress towards overall goals and the completion of larger goals down the road.
- Set realistic deadlines for your contributing team members and hold everyone accountable for meeting them.
- Make the process fun for everyone involved! Creating a volunteer management plan offers a great opportunity to bond and collaborate with your team.
- During the planning process, don't forget to leverage your volunteers and their desired outcomes of the program.

DEVELOP A STRATEGY TO MEET YOUR GOALS

Once your organization has developed an outline of your program's goals and timeline, you'll need to determine how your plan will reach those goals. Take your time and do the homework while developing these strategies. Remember, yours is not the first organization to create a strategic volunteer management program; leverage the problem areas and solutions that other organizations have identified during their own volunteer program development efforts. Many of these assets can be found online; let's look at a few best practices on the implementation level.

One aspect of volunteer management that your organization will want to focus on is recruitment and role development. We will discuss volunteer recruitment strategies in more detail in the next chapter, but it is important identify recruitment as a component of plan creation and a best practice to remain aware of throughout the implementation process. When laying the foundation of your plan, you will have asked yourself, "What are the key roles your organization is hoping to attract volunteers to fill?" Once that question is answered, you will need to create an appealing role description and take steps toward finding the right candidate to fill that opportunity. Here are a few questions to consider while creating opportunity descriptions:

- What are volunteers expected to achieve in an organizational role?
- What are the boundaries of the role and opportunity?
- How will the opportunity be supervised? How will your organization prepare supervisors for the opportunity fulfillment?
- What support will your organization provide to volunteers in this opportunity?
- Where will volunteers fulfill the opportunity? Will they have access to the resources they need to be successful?
- What resources are needed to efficiently and successfully fulfill the opportunity?
- How many hours will it take for a volunteer to fulfil a specific opportunity successfully? Can the opportunity be accomplished by part-time volunteers?
- Are there any opportunities to enrich the professional lives of volunteers in this role?
- What skills and characteristics should a volunteer possess to be successful in this opportunity?

Identifying the primary roles your organization needs to fill and creating a detailed job description for those roles based on your program vision is a great way to begin to identify who your ideal volunteer prospect is. Only then will you be able to create personas and recruitment strategies that target this audience specifically.

It's also important to remember that your nonprofit's supporters are one of your organization's most important assets. Supporters can lead to referrals, which can then lead to the fulfillment of opportunities and, over time, new supporters. Focusing on the development of lifelong supporters can assist your nonprofit in its quest of retaining talent in the long-run. As a best practice, your volunteer management plan should focus on creating an environment that produces repeat volunteers. Many nonprofits today struggle with finding prospects to fill volunteer roles, but even more organizations are challenged with the ability to retain talent once they've found it. While we will discuss volunteer retention in much more detail in chapter 6, here are a few retention-related questions to consider while creating your volunteer management program:

- How is your organization going to communicate exciting opportunities to your current volunteer-base?
- How does your nonprofit plan to provide supporters with updates regarding current goals and attainment of your organization's mission?
- What steps will your organization take to excite your target audience about your nonprofit's brand?
- How will your organization tap into your target prospects' emotions? What stories will you tell?
- How does your nonprofit plan to keep supporters engaged, both in the short-term and long-term?
- What additional value can your organization bring to the lives of supporters?
- What incentives, rewards, and recognition can your organization offer supporters in exchange for their commitment?
- What is causing your nonprofit's current volunteers to fill only one opportunity? Is there a trend that can be addressed?
- How will your volunteer management plan track volunteer retention rates? How will that data be used to make your appeal stronger?
- How will your organization leverage the skills and strengths of volunteers to give its supporters purpose?
- What steps will your organization take to stay in touch and follow up with supporters regarding their volunteer experience?

The process of creating a volunteer management strategy that assists your organization in reaching its goals should be specific, measurable, attainable, realistic, and timely. A volunteer management process is a worthwhile investment that will provide your organization with invaluable insights into the strengths, weaknesses, and opportunities of your volunteer program. If your organization is interested in making volunteer data collection easier, gaining visibility into how that data interacts, improving the communication process, strengthening recruitment efforts, and streamlining management as a whole, it may be the right time to consider adding a volunteer management software solution to your toolset.

WHAT IS VOLUNTEER MANAGEMENT SOFTWARE AND WHAT ARE THE BENEFITS?

Volunteer management software is a tool that can greatly streamline your efforts when implementing a volunteer management plan and process. Volunteer management solutions are packed with features, including specialized communication tools, online registration and scheduling capabilities, and true CRM integration functionality, just to name a few. Let's discuss a few of the key benefits of volunteer management software in more detail.

The most basic and key functionality attained through volunteer management software is the capability to allow volunteers to self-schedule, a feature that enables prospects to view a real-time schedule of volunteer opportunities online and simply register for those activities that best fit those volunteers' interests. This gives your volunteers greater visibility into your nonprofit's needs and goals, while also allowing volunteers the ability to compare those needs with their own personal skillsets and availability without first having to reach out to a coordinator. As a result, efficiencies within the key areas of your volunteer program soar.

In addition to improving the efficiency of your program in general through volunteer self-scheduling, there are a number of key administrative benefits that can only be attained through the implementation of volunteer management software. These benefits can have a drastic impact on your nonprofit's recruitment strategy, the first of which is the ability to free up more of your volunteer coordinator's time. Here are just a handful of the ways that volunteer management software can help volunteer coordinators with more effective time management:

- Easily organize and access your nonprofit's real-time volunteer data from anywhere.
- Build and automate processes, including your organization's volunteer communication efforts.
- Integrate your volunteer data with your nonprofit's CRM system to help streamline task assignment at an organizational level.
- Integrate with Google Analytics to give your nonprofit better insights into volunteerism and engagement trends.

One of the most important features of volunteer management software that is often overlooked is the ability to communicate with volunteers more effectively. Notifications can help your nonprofit keep volunteers up-to-date regarding an opportunity they've signed up for, new opportunities that are available, appreciation for a volunteer who recently provided their time, and the nonprofit's current efforts towards a cause. Communicating frequently and effectively with your volunteers can have a large impact on a nonprofit's ability to retain volunteers and improve opportunity turn-out.

Another notable feature of volunteer management software is the benefit of being able to attract and retain volunteers in a multitude of ways. The most effective volunteer management solutions allow nonprofit organizations to create custom-branded pages for various volunteer opportunities. These opportunities can be shared across marketing platforms such as your nonprofit's website and social media accounts to increase visibility. Another benefit of being able to create these unique landing pages using volunteer management software is the ability to segment your outreach initiatives. Volunteer coordinators can easily access and share multiple opportunity pages at the same time as well as simplify group volunteerism with special co-branded opportunity pages. This feature makes it easier for organizations to achieve their volunteer recruitment goals while focusing on time management.

Another opportunity that volunteer management software can provide to nonprofits is an increased ability to convert volunteers to donors. Volunteers have already shown interest in the nonprofit's mission and values, making them the perfect candidate to solicit for financial contributions. Did you know that 42% of volunteers also give?[31] Your nonprofit should always be tapping into its volunteer base in its quest for donors; incorporating the right volunteer management software can greatly assist in your conversion goals.

Here are a few ways a volunteer management solution can help:

- Volunteer management software allows a nonprofit to track all volunteer activity.
- Acknowledgments through notifications go a long way in creating cheerleaders for your cause.
- Volunteer management helps to identify who to ask for donations based on their organizational involvement.
- Integrated software can improve transparency within your organization and improve organization efforts for your volunteer program and nonprofit as a whole.

Incorporating volunteer management software into your organization's volunteer processes is a great way to see and understand trends within your volunteer program and make adjustments based on real data. Volunteer management software also provides many efficiencies through self-registration and communication features that can help in attracting and retaining supporters both in the short-term and in the long-term. Finding the right solution can take an enormous stress off your organization's staff and completely eliminate inefficient, paper-based management efforts.

Converting volunteers to donors is an immense and often unrealized opportunity for nonprofits that we will explore further in the next chapter.

A BRIDGE BETWEEN VOLUNTEERS AND FINANCIAL DONORS

"Every person can make a difference, and every person should try."

—John F. Kennedy

I t is easy to see how important volunteers are for nonprofits to realize their mission and goals. Organizations utilize volunteer hours and the fulfillment of opportunities to help make the community a better place. However, a large number of volunteers also provide nonprofits with additional value; outside of offering their time in the form of volunteerism, many believe enough in the issues being addressed to donate financial resources to the cause. In fact, according to a study, two-thirds of volunteers donate monetary assets to the same organization to which they donate their time.[32] Financial donations provided by volunteers are, on average, *10 times higher* than non-volunteer donations.[33] Many attribute the higher donation amount provided by volunteers to their direct experience working with an organization to fulfill its mission.

A direct correlation exists between the number of opportunities a volunteer fills and the amount that same volunteer donates financially to a cause. On average, the more time a person spends volunteering, the higher the financial contribution they will commit. This statistic reflects the importance of turning volunteers into lifelong supporters. It also reinforces the importance of volunteers and the need to convert volunteer prospects to donors. So, what steps can your organization take to increase cross-pollination opportunities and covert more of its volunteers to financial donors?

Let's explore the similarities between volunteers and donors and the five key strategies to increase volunteer-to-donor conversion rates.

SIMILARITIES BETWEEN VOLUNTEER AND DONOR MOTIVES

There are many similarities between volunteers and donors that make them both great candidates for cross-pollination. First, both volunteers and donors believe in philanthropic activity and have a desire to support the greater-good – they have proven this desire through their contributions over time. In addition, both groups believe in the mission and goals your organization is hoping to achieve; otherwise, they would not be so willing to give to your unique cause.

Another similarity between volunteers and donors is the need to be nurtured and recognized for their contributions in order to be retained in the future. Current donor retention rates in the United States average just above 40% today, while volunteer retention rates are substantially higher, averaging between 50% and 70% depending on the state.[34] These statistics demonstrate the increased value your organization can obtain by converting financial donors to volunteers. Furthermore, both volunteers and donors want to see that their contribution is being used efficiently and effectively.

Finally, volunteers and donors both have the power to provide your organization with crucial information in the form of feedback. That feedback on their experience with your nonprofit can pave the way for future improvements to your volunteer program and donor management efforts as well as provide an initial glimpse at ways for your organization to bridge the gap between the two.

VOLUNTEER AND DONOR DEMOGRAPHICS

As discussed in chapter three, people volunteer for a plethora of reasons. To convert more volunteers to donors, it is crucial to understand who the average volunteer is. While your volunteer data may paint a different picture of who that person is for your organization, there are some interesting insights that can be gathered from average volunteer statistics.

According to a study performed by The Bureau of Labor Statistics, 45% of the U.S. population volunteers.[35] Individuals between the ages of 35 and 54 are most likely to volunteer, representing just under 60% of the total volunteers in the U.S. in 2015. Woman are more likely to volunteer than men by about 6%, while a higher education level has also been shown to increase the likelihood of a person providing their time to a cause. According to the study, 71% of volunteers have had some college experience or received a degree prior to becoming involved in volunteerism. In addition, individuals who are employed are 5% more likely to volunteer than individuals who are between jobs.

Now let's look at the average financial donor. Understanding your donors is key if you hope to cross-pollinate donors with volunteers and increase their involvement in your cause. Based on giving as a whole in the U.S., year-over-year financial giving continues to rise. In 2016, financial donations reached $390 billion dollars; this figure is seven times higher than recorded financial contributions in 1954 according to an industry study.[36] Individual donors make up the largest percentage of monetary giving, representing 71% of all financial donations. Understanding the average donor making up this 71% is therefore paramount, and many trends have been captured regarding the average donor and the causes that are driving the most monetary support.

The most financially supported causes as of 2018 are religious, education, and human services. According to a study, 64% of all financial donations are made by woman, while 36% were made by men.[37] Digging deeper into the average U.S. donor reveals that Generation X donors are most likely to give more than once per year (50%), followed closely by baby boomers (47%). Education level and income also have an impact on donor behavior; the percentage of people giving rises as income level rises in the U.S. According to a study performed by Philanthropy Roundtable, 37% of families making $25,000 or less give financially to charity, whereas 93% of families who make 162,000 a year donated financially to a cause.[38] Education is also a factor in terms of the desire and ability to give financially. Individuals who have a bachelor's degree are 1.5 times more likely to give than those who do not.

CLOSING THE GAP

As illustrated by the above data, average volunteer and donor metrics can relate in several areas. Both financial and time donations appear to increase as income and education levels increase. Women represent the highest demographic in both categories. Finally, individuals between the ages of 30 and 60 appear to be the most likely to both volunteer and donate financially.

That said, these numbers are purely average statistics and will not necessarily reflect your organization's targeting; your target should be based solely on your organization's donor and volunteer statistics. Once your nonprofit has determined who your volunteers and donors are, you can begin to deploy cross-pollination tactics.

PERSONALIZE YOUR PROSPECTS' EXPERIENCE

Remember, converting volunteers to donors starts by providing volunteers with a great experience. Creating a personalized experience demonstrates to supporters that your nonprofit is organized and cares about their individual contributions to the cause. Personalization needs to be incorporated in outreach, training, opportunity fulfillment, and follow-up communications. A study performed by HubSpot in 2014 found that 70% of people get frustrated when outreach content isn't relevant to them and their relationship with the organization.[39] Personalization should be used to make your supporters feel special and lead them toward a specific action based on their individual preferences.

Organizations can use personalization to convert volunteers to donors by delivering content that a specific supporter is most interested in based on past behavior, rekindling the emotions that triggered a supporter's involvement, and answering questions that may be blocking a supporter from additional involvement.

Nonprofits can personalize their outreach, training, and opportunity fulfillment efforts in the following ways:

- Create targeted pages for volunteer opportunities that focus on specific visitor attributes. These pages may also present an additional opportunity to promote fundraising.
- Send personalized emails and text notifications reminding volunteers of upcoming opportunities and thanking them for their previous engagements. Personalized communications are another avenue for cross-promoting fundraising.
- Promote value to volunteers in the form of career development, networking, skill-building and community support. Demonstrating additional value can entice a volunteer to also become a donor in an effort to support your organization's program.
- Tell stories of hope and change that tug at the emotions of your volunteers. As discussed previously, emotional response is one of the best ways to increase a volunteer's involvement in the cause.
- Personalize training material to demonstrate the value your organization sees in each volunteer. Demonstrating the value your organization places on each volunteer can help those volunteers become more invested (emotionally and, over time, financially) in supporting your cause.

ACKNOWLEDGE PARTICIPATION AND ACCOMPLISHMENTS

Acknowledging volunteer participation and accomplishments is another great way to promote donor conversions from existing supporters. Appreciation can increase the likelihood that a volunteer will become an even larger supporter in the future and add financial donations to their contributions. Nonprofits need to treat their volunteer-base the same way they treat current financial donors. Let volunteers see the impact that their time commitment is making in the community.

Here are a few examples of communications demonstrating appreciation to volunteers for their contributions:

- "Thank you for volunteering with our organization. The four hours you provided made a substantial impact on our continued efforts to support the community. Because of your support, we were able to feed an additional 150 families!"
- "The fundraising assistance you provided to our organization allowed us to receive $15,000 in donations. These funds will help us to serve 250 more families throughout the community this year. Thank you for your support and the difference you helped us make!"
- "Your recent contribution as a volunteer has allowed us to provide shelter for a family in need. Volunteers like you are helping our organization to create reliable housing for 300 families a year. Thank you so much for your continued support."
- "Thank you for fulling a recent volunteer shift with our organization. Because of your commitment, we were able to send out 1,000 donation requests, resulting in $5000 dollars in new donations. These donations will have a positive impact on the lives of 10,000 people in the community!"

Recognizing participation by communicating personal impact can provide volunteers with transparent and quantifiable results of their commitment. These communications may also translate volunteer fulfillment into a dollar amount raised or the number of people served, making the message even more powerful for the volunteer. Finally, by showing the impact of how fundraising is helping the community, your organization could entice a volunteer to donate financially as well.

DON'T UNDERESTIMATE THE POWER OF AN "ASK"

Sometimes converting a volunteer into a donor is as simple as asking them for financial support. Many nonprofit organizations fear that asking volunteers for monetary donations on top of their time is too much to request. However, data suggests that volunteers are 10 times more likely to give financially than non-volunteers. Most volunteers are also heavily invested in supporting your organization's cause and therefore will do what they can to ensure the obtainment of your organization's mission. Asking a volunteer to donate is a good strategy to increase donor conversions, but there are a few best practices to consider when making the "ask":

- Base the ask on emotion and clearly define a goal for the funding request.
- Provide real-world examples of how financial contributions are making a positive impact on the community and your organization's mission.
- Don't be aggressive. If volunteers are not interested after the initial ask, thank them for their consideration and move on.
- Provide volunteers with the specific amount you are requesting.Create digital opportunities for your volunteers to give without a direct ask. We'll discuss this further in the next section.

MAKE GIVING AS EASY AS POSSIBLE

Technology is making the process of asking for donations and giving donations easier for all parties involved. If your digital presence is not working on your organization's behalf by making giving as easy as possible for potential donors, then your nonprofit is missing out on a substantial opportunity.

An easy way to make giving easier is by investing and optimizing your organization's website for user experience and convertibility. Here are a few optimizations to promote the ease of giving:

- Make your website fundraising calls to action clear, concise, and actionable.
- Eliminate any distractions that could be taking website visitors away from a fundraising call to action.
- Eliminate any unnecessary "clicks" that may be blocking conversions or dragging out the conversion process.
- Make sure your website, donation pages, and calls to action are optimized across browsing platforms (i.e., mobile, desktop, tablet) and operating systems (i.e., Mac, Windows, Linux).
- Include a suggested gift amount and an impact statement.
- Offer donors a recurring gift option to increase donor retention rates.
- Promote channel streams so that donors can stay in touch and continue to learn about how your organization supports the community. Collect web traffic and user experience analytics and continue to optimize your online fundraising efforts based on those findings.

INTEGRATE VOLUNTEER AND DONOR TECHNOLOGY

As discussed in Chapter 4, investing in volunteer management software is a significant way to streamline the process of communicating opportunities, filling them, and retaining your supporters. Another benefit of volunteer management software is the ability to integrate it with your nonprofit's donor software solution and database.

Integrating your volunteer and donor technology can help increase your organization's awareness of cross-pollination opportunities by bridging the gap between data sets. The result is an opportunity to gain better understanding of your current volunteers who donate both time and financial resources to the cause, which you can then use to drive your efforts to convert more volunteers to donors (and vice-versa).

Integrating your volunteer management system with your donor platform can give your nonprofit the opportunity to:

- Bridge the gap between your development and volunteer management teams and strategies by granting them transparency into each other's processes.
- Increase viable donor candidates significantly by soliciting to an existing but otherwise untapped pipeline of prospects.
- Cross-pollinate your organization's communications to solicit donors for their time toward your cause and volunteers for financial contributions.
- Grant easy access to your organizations fundraising and volunteer opportunities to a much broader audience to increase your nonprofit's potential reach and impact.

Greatly increase the potential of long-term contributions made by both volunteers and donors by allowing them to become involved in more ways than one.

MARKETING STRATEGIES TO ATTRACT TODAY'S VOLUNTEERS

"Success comes from standing out, not fitting in."

– Don Draper

Many nonprofits today struggle with the ability to attract new talent to fill crucial organizational roles. As you now know, volunteerism has been on the rise over the past several years, so we can conclude that those nonprofits' struggles are not due to a lack of individuals willing to provide their time in exchange for making a positive difference. Reaching these individuals, however, can be challenging if an organization has not developed a strategy for marketing and opportunity outreach. In this chapter, we will examine several best practices for marketing to today's volunteers.

EMAIL, CONTENT, AND SOCIAL MARKETING STATISTICS

Before discussing individual marketing strategies to drive qualified prospects, let's first examine some basic nonprofit marketing statistics for the industry. These statistics demonstrate the shift we have seen in nonprofit marketing over the years, missed opportunities, and where industry marketing is heading in the future.

Nonprofit Industry (US)	All Industries (US)
EMAIL MARKETING	
• The average open rate for nonprofit email marketing campaigns is 25.96%.[40] • The average click-through rate on nonprofit email campaigns is 8%.[41] • The average nonprofit misses out on around $14,000 annually due to emails being classified as spam. • 37% of nonprofits do not send follow-up emails to new online subscribers within 30 days. • Nonprofit email lists grew an average of 10% in 2016.[42]	• The national average for email open rates across all industries is 21.73% (4.23% less than average nonprofit rate).[43] • The national average for email click-through rates is 3.57% (less than half the nonprofit average). • On average, email lists naturally decay by 22.5% each year.[44] • Segmented email campaigns are more likely to be opened than non-segmented campaigns.[45] • About 53% of all emails are opened on mobile devices.[46]
CONTENT MARKETING	
• 92% of nonprofit organizations use content marketing as a substantial part of their marketing mix.[47] • 54% of nonprofit marketers struggle with measuring content effectiveness. • 42% of nonprofits find it challenging to produce engaging content on a regular basis.[48]	• 57% of marketers say custom content is their top marketing priority. • Content marketing receives three times the leads per dollar invested compared with paid search.[50] • 60% of marketers create one or more pieces of new content each day.[51]

- Only 29% of nonprofits reuse and repurpose existing content
- Only 23% of nonprofits have a documented content marketing strategy.[49]

- Content marketing costs 62% less than traditional marketing.[52]
- 37% of business-to-business marketers have a written content strategy (14% more than nonprofits).[53]

SOCIAL MEDIA MARKETING

- Facebook is currently the most used social media marketing site by U.S. charities and nonprofits.[54] In addition, 98% of nonprofit organizations have a Facebook page.
- 83% of nonprofits are on Twitter, while only 40% use Instagram.
- 55% of millennials prefer to learn about nonprofits via social media.[55]
- 41% of nonprofits attribute social media success to a detailed strategy.[56] 47% of Americans learn about causes via social media and online channels.

- 22% of the world's population uses Facebook.
- Instagram is the second most popular social media site in the U.S., while Twitter comes in as the fourth most popular social media site.
- Twitter has less than half the number of users as Facebook.
- Snapchat reaches 41% of 18-34-year olds daily.[57]
- YouTube reaches more 18-49-year olds than any cable network in the U.S.[58]
- 80% of time spent on social media is done on a mobile device.

The above statistics outline metrics surrounding several of the most prevalent marketing channels in the nonprofit space today. Email, content, and social media marketing are cost-effective platforms that can reach the masses and elicit new supporters on a large scale. These statistics also communicate the importance of having a clear-cut strategy when using any of these channels to recruit and engage with prospects. The marketing channels your organization uses to target your ideal audience depends on your mission, goals, and resources available. If your organization is new to marketing, you might begin by investing in email, content, and social media marketing.

Let's take a more detailed look into several strategies for getting the most benefit out of email, content, and social media marketing for your nonprofit organization.

EMAIL MARKETING TO REACH SUPPORTERS

Email is still one of the most effective forms of marketing today, even in our inbound marketing world. Organizations that leverage email campaigns in their nonprofit marketing have a better chance of attracting new donors and volunteers than their counterparts. So the question becomes, "How can a nonprofit create a marketing campaign that drives their organization forward and does not become just another unread email in a potential volunteer's or donor's inbox?"

This section will explore a few tactics that your organization can utilize to create more successful email marketing campaigns and take your nonprofit marketing strategy to new heights. However, it's first important to understand why email is still a relevant channel for nonprofit marketing:

- Email marketing is one of the most cost-effective forms of marketing.
- Email marketing reaches mobile audiences with ease.
- Email is estimated to reach 3 billion users by 2020.
- The success rate of email marketing campaigns is easily measured and optimized.

These benefits easily demonstrate why email is still an effective approach to recruiting and engaging volunteers. Now let's take a look at specific strategies you can easily apply to your volunteer program.

FOCUS YOUR EMAIL STRATEGY ON A CLEAR OBJECTIVE

Before creating an email campaign, it is key that your organization identifies and understands its objectives. In other words, what action do you want your recipients to take? What do you want the result of your efforts to be?

Understanding your organization's objectives will clarify each email campaign's purpose and make the call to action more effective. Your nonprofit organization should take some time to brainstorm these objectives and determine the outcome that best coincides with its mission, values, and goals.

CREATE A COMPELLING EMAIL SUBJECT

The subject line is one of the most important components of a successful email marketing campaign. Did you know that 33% of email recipients decide whether or not to open an email based on the subject line?[59] The email's subject is your opportunity to capture the reader with a powerful "first impression," since the subject line is the first snippet of information that your nonprofit's target audience will see before making the decision to open or delete the email. Creating a compelling subject line is therefore crucial to the success of your nonprofit marketing objectives.

Here are a few tips for creating a more compelling email subject:

- **Keep the subject line short and sweet.** Many inboxes will truncate longer subjects, and readers often make the decision to continue reading after just a few words.
- **Make your subject line action-oriented.** Starting your subject with a verb like "engage" or "improve" can often help you hook a reader's interest.
- **Give insights on what the email content is about.** In addition, try to align your subject with your objective when possible.
- **Create a sense of urgency.** Many times, introducing a deadline can help drive readers to click to avoid missing out on a "limited opportunity."
- **Incorporate personalization.** Make your subject line grab your readers' attention by ensuring it captures what they really care about.

SEGMENT EMAIL LISTS BY VOLUNTEER/DONOR INTERESTS

Creating personalized email marketing campaigns is becoming a more important campaign success factor than ever before. The best way your nonprofit can create personalized campaigns is to focus on your email lists so messages are more relevant to your audience. Take the time to understand each of your email contacts and what offers and opportunities they are most interested in. Once you identify this information, segmenting your email efforts becomes a lot easier.

Here are a few tips on how to segment your email lists:

- Fully understand the past engagement of each of your email contacts, such as the types of activities they've participated in, the fundraising efforts they've contributed to, the causes they've expressed interest in, etc.
- Leverage analytics to identify audience website behavior, such as the pages they've accessed most frequently.
- Create personas using the data in your volunteer and donor databases.
- Break down your email lists by organizational role or status.
- Analyze past email campaign initiatives to see which subjects specific people are interested in based on previous behavior.
- Survey your email lists to find out what information your audiences would be most interested in learning about as well as how working with your organization can provide value to those individuals.

PERSONALIZE EMAIL CONTENT

When marketers talk about creating personalized email content, people often associate the action with creating a name field. While using your contact's name within the body of the email is one good way to provide personalization, this is only part of what your nonprofit can do to provide a more customized experience for each reader. There is plenty of functionality that email platforms can provide around personalization, and the ability to integrate with other tools is endless.

Here are a few personalization tactics your organization should incorporate into your nonprofit marketing strategy to increase the click rate of your email marketing campaigns:

- Create behavioral email triggers based on a prospect's interaction with your nonprofit's website.
- Consider the prospect's geographic location and time zone when deciding on the best time to email them.
- Deliver specific content based on what prospects have been interested in in the past.
- Include the prospect's name in the subject line.
- Think of your demographic when choosing appropriate email imagery.
- Use personalization tags and dynamic content.

CREATE THE RIGHT AMOUNT OF COPY

There is a fine line between having too much and too little content in an email marketing campaign. You do not want to draw your target audience's attention away from the objective that you identified as the primary call to action. One best practice is to focus your efforts on the visual appeal of the email and limit the amount of content to a minimum. Keep in mind that less is often more, and you only have a limited amount of time to deliver your primary message to your audience.

Here are a few best practices when crafting email copy:

- Correct spelling and grammar can make all the difference in converting prospects.
- Keep your emails under 750 words in length (content that is too long will end up in the spam folder). You can always save some of the extra content for a new campaign later.

- Format your email to fit all device types and have a consistent design across email platforms. Many tools are available online to help you test your designs across browsers and platforms almost instantly.
- Choose a font that is easily readable. In addition, avoid a multitude of font colors, styles and sizes, as they can be distracting or difficult for some people to read.

DEVELOP A SUBSCRIPTION PROCESS

Building the process of subscribing (and unsubscribing) into an email campaign often scares nonprofits. They want to gain new contacts but do not want to take the chance of losing existing email list connections. However, this concern introduces the risk of your emails being flagged as spam, and you may lose your ability to use an email platform altogether as a result. It is much better to give your connections the ability to unsubscribe easily to avoid them reporting your email as spam if they feel receiving your nonprofit's correspondence was not justified or relevant to them. Your emails should always contain an easy-to-find link or instructions to unsubscribe.

That said, one way to limit the amount of unsubscribes and spam reports is to build your email list *organically*. In other words, find your own prospects; do not fall into the trap of purchasing an email list. Your best possible audience consists of the people who have opted to receive your emails in the past. You'll have a much better chance of converting these home-grown prospects, so focus your efforts on providing unique actionable content.

TEST AND OPTIMIZE EMAIL CAMPAIGNS

Optimizing your nonprofit's marketing efforts based on both previous successes and past failures are one of the most important factors in determining the impact an email campaign will have on your organization. Creating an email campaign is only the first step in achieving the positive results your nonprofit hopes to achieve, and any nonprofit organization has access to the basic tools necessary for testing the effectiveness of email campaign components. Chances are the email campaign tool you already use can analyze campaign results. In addition, free tools like Google Analytics can help you track the effects of your email efforts on traffic and conversion rates in your website.

Email is still one of the most effective forms of nonprofit marketing. When done right, email campaigns can deliver a high return on investment (ROI) and create a list of followers organically. Remember to focus on the primary action you want to drive your audience to take. Spend time optimizing your campaigns based on real data and how your audience has interacted with your campaigns in the past. Use the free tools that are available online to make better optimization decisions and promote conversion increases. Email is — and will continue to be — a relevant and affordable way to reach potential volunteers and donors.

CONTENT MARKETING TO REACH SUPPORTERS

Focusing part of your marketing strategy around content creation and publication is a great way to reach and drive interest in your nonprofit's mission and goals. Many marketers today have found success in developing and deploying a content marketing strategy that appeals to their target prospects. As shown in the statistics at the beginning of this chapter, content marketing is a cost-effective way to drive qualified leads. The most common examples of online content marketing include blogging and social media posts.

The issue many nonprofits face today is the ability to run effective content strategies that deliver an ROI in while having access to limited resources. Nonprofits that are successful in content creation are creating compelling content pieces that tell stories of impact. Below are a few ways your organization can create a content strategy that delivers results.

CREATE CONTENT THAT SOLVES A PROBLEM OR DELIVERS A NEED

Creating content that your prospects want to engage with begins by identifying a problem or a need. Content should always address the question, "How can we help?" Identifying topics that will interest your target audience begins by truly understanding who your audience is and what motivates them to give time and resources to a cause. Once your organization understands its target audience and the problems those prospects are facing, it will be much easier to create channels for that content that appeal to them.

Here are a few tips for creating content that solves a problem:

- Get to know your prospects and their problems and build content that provides solutions to those problems.
- Talk to current volunteers and donors to understand what motivates them specifically to give to your organization.
- Leverage social media and your community to find topics of interest.
- Do keyword research to see what specific keywords are driving visitors to your site.
- Analyze your organization's previous content and develop new content based on topics that your prospects were previously interested in.
- Create content that targets a specific niche audience (for instance, based on personas).
- Make your content resonate on an emotional level with prospects.
- See what topics similar organizations are writing about by visiting their websites and social media or by using free analytics tools like BuzzSumo.

ALWAYS HAVE A CALL TO ACTION

Your calls to action (CTAs) should guide prospects to perform a specific action. In other words, once someone reads your content, what is it you want them to *do*? Your organization may want to use content to find potential volunteers or donors or push prospects to another piece of content. Mapping out CTAs and how they work with your content to achieve a common goal is crucial to the success of your content strategy. In order for content marketing to be successful, your organization needs to create *copy with purpose.*

Here are a few tips for creating more actionable and relevant CTAs:

- Make sure your CTA is clear and concise. The more likely a reader is to understand your CTA, the more likely they are to act on it.
- Don't expect your prospects to dig for your CTA. Make it extremely easy to find.
- Be specific regarding what you want prospects to do. Should they click a link, call someone or fill out a form? Drive them directly to their next step as clearly as possible.
- Use A/B testing to try various approaches to your content CTAs and identify potential opportunities for improvement.
- Ensure your CTAs create a sense of value for the volunteers or financial donors your organization is trying to recruit by identifying what's in it for your supporters.

REPURPOSE EXISTING CONTENT AND COLLATERAL

Many nonprofit organizations fail to realize the enormous potential of existing content, which can be repurposed later to engage new audiences across different channels. Using the same content in a multitude of ways can help organizations that lack time, staff, and resources to devote to full-time content creation. That said, not all content is reusable; it's important to remember that content should only be repurposed if it helps your prospects solve a problem or answer a question. Content that is outdated needs to be updated prior to repurposing, and analytics on previous content can help your organization identify whether or not it's worth repurposing.

Here are a few ways you can repurpose existing content to reach new audiences:

- Transform recorded webinars into rewatchable YouTube videos.

- Convert internal data such as surveys and notes into case studies.
- Repost photos on social media sites such as Pinterest or Facebook.
- Turn blog posts into infographics or short social media posts.
- Promote blog content in a weekly newsletter email campaign.
- Transform blog posts into podcasts to attract an audio audience.

SOCIAL MEDIA MARKETING TO REACH SUPPORTERS

Using social media strategically can also help attract prospects and build a community around a cause. As mentioned earlier, social media sites often have more traffic and provide more visibility than traditional marketing outlets, and at a fraction of the cost. Social media and storytelling also go hand in hand, which makes the channel a natural place for nonprofits to promote their mission. However, success on social media requires a nonprofit to have a strategy, the ability to allocate resources, and an understanding of ROI measurement.

Here are a few questions to consider when developing a social strategy:

- What is social media's role in your organization's current communications strategy?
- What does your organization want social media to accomplish?
- Who is your target audience and in what social media platforms do they spend their time?
- Do you base your social presence, content theme and tone on the question above?
- How frequently do you need to post to keep your audience engaged?
- When is the best time to post content to your channels?
- How will you empower your advocates to cross-promote content?
- How will your organization track and measure results?

Where you spend your time on social media should come down to where your prospects spend there time. Investing time in the channels that your prospects enjoy most will make the process of building a community easier. You may or may not find that your results are similar to that of other nonprofits as well as to industry averages.

MOST POPULAR SOCIAL MEDIA CHANNELS IN NONPROFIT SECTOR

A recent survey of 9,000 small-to-medium sized nonprofits in the United States recorded which social networks those nonprofits used most frequently to engage prospects.[60] The results of that survey provide a glimpse at the social media presence of the nonprofit sector as a whole:

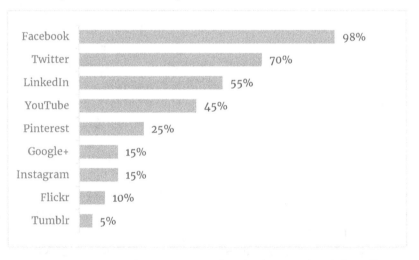

Channel	Percentage
Facebook	98%
Twitter	70%
LinkedIn	55%
YouTube	45%
Pinterest	25%
Google+	15%
Instagram	15%
Flickr	10%
Tumblr	5%

Remember, however, that your organization's use of social media may or may not align with the above averages. Again, which social media platforms your organization chooses to utilize should focus more on your prospects' social media activity.

LEVERAGING SOCIAL MEDIA TO CREATE OPPORTUNITY

If used correctly, social media offers a lot of benefits to nonprofits. Organizations can use social media to broadcast their messaging cost-effectively. However, without a clear plan and strategic execution, social media marketing can actually become more work and investment than the return. As with any marketing channel, there are several best practices to consider when using social media to promote your nonprofit's mission, goals, and cause.

Here are a few tips to consider:

- Create a process for keeping track of what people in the community are saying about your nonprofit and volunteer program.
- Keep your messaging consistent and concise across channels.
- Make shared content engaging for volunteers and prospects. Use social as an opportunity to create real relationships.
- Empower staff and supporters to be brand advocates and self-promote content.
- Have a plan to deal with negative feedback.
- Provide a clear call to action for each post and track results.
- Define and track your organization's target ROI for social media.

When incorporating these new strategies into your organization's marketing mix, be sure that your marketing has a clear focus and goal for your prospects. Remember that sometimes, less is more.

Now that you understand the various marketing strategies and outlets used by most nonprofits, it's time to dive into some specific tips and tricks for tracking your marketing and outreach initiatives.

TRACKING THE SUCCESS OF VOLUNTEER PROGRAM MARKETING

"Marketers have to stop reporting on activities and start reporting on business outcomes."

– Allen Gannett

As discussed previously, marketing your nonprofit's volunteer opportunities across many different channels, such as content, social media, email and your organization's website, is essential. Marketing your volunteer opportunities is important if your nonprofit wants to drive in qualified volunteer prospects. In order to optimize those marketing efforts, it is crucial to track results and make strategy adjustments based on successes and failures.

In this chapter, we will focus on ways your nonprofit can monitor and report marketing progress. Remember that it is key to have marketing objectives for each channel identified before attempting to measure and report key performance indicators (KPIs), or more simply put, those values that help demonstrate the level of success your organization is achieving for a particular objective. A good place to start is by determining your volunteer program's overall marketing goals and KPIs for each of its marketing channels.

VOLUNTEER PROGRAM MARKETING GOALS & KPI'S

Determining the overall goals and KPIs for your volunteer program's marketing efforts is the first step your nonprofit should take before creating a system for measuring each channel. Doing so will allow your nonprofit to create KPIs for each channel that aligns with its overall goals.

Some of the most common goals for marketing a volunteer program include:

- Increasing opportunity fulfillment
- Increasing prospect network and program visibility
- Standing out from other causes by creating content and collateral that is highly engageable
- Increasing total volunteer inquiries each month
- Improving retention rates through online engagement with supporters
- Converting volunteers to donors
- Re-engaging volunteers who have not fulfilled opportunities recently

Choosing your marketing KPIs should then be unique to your organization and what your nonprofit is hoping to achieve. Next, the following strategic questions can help when deciding on your marketing goals:

- What are your volunteer program's short-term and long-term goals?
- What KPIs are necessary to sustain your organization's volunteer program?
- What channels has your organization used in the past? What goals did they reach?

- Is your organization in alignment regarding program goals?
- Are the goals you have outlined SMART (specific, measurable, assignable, realistic and time-related)?
- Do your goals impact the bottom line? Do you have supporting goals?
- Are your goals in line with your organization's mission and values?
- Have you created and documented a detailed plan outlining these objectives?

Once your organization has determined its overall marketing goals, it's time to choose marketing channels strategically to drive your organization closer to fulfilling them. The ultimate goal of all channels should be to provide your nonprofit with value. Remember to consider the time necessary to manage and optimize a channel successfully as an investment when determining ROI, even if you are using a channel organically (rather than paying for channel ad space).

Next, let's take a closer look at common KPIs for each of the marketing channels discussed previously: email, social media, and content marketing.

EMAIL MARKETING KPI'S

Email marketing has the power to be an incredibly effective channel if measured and optimized strategically. In fact, email is more effective in the nonprofit space than in any other industry. As discussed previously, the average open rate for nonprofit emails is 25.96%, much higher than the universal open rate of 6% across all industries. What a staggering difference!

If your organization wants to reap the rewards of an effective email marketing strategy, there are a number of specific KPIs you should measure and report.

- **Campaign Click-Through Rates** are the percentage of people who engaged with (clicked) one or more links in an email. This measurement demonstrates interaction. By measuring click-through rates, your organization can see which emails most resonated and sparked action with your volunteer and/or prospect audience.

- **Bounce Rates** are the percentage of emails that are not successfully delivered to recipients. Having too many bounced emails suggests that a campaign list may need to be scrubbed or examined for quality. Measuring bounce rates can help your nonprofit remove unengaged subscribers from email lists and demonstrate to email providers that you are reputable.

- **Spam Rates** are the percentage of recipients that report emails as unsolicited. High spam rates imply that your contacts did not agree to receive your correspondence or deemed the content irrelevant to them. If your spam rates are high, you run the risk of losing the ability to send emails with an email provider in the future.

- **Growth Rates** are the number of new subscribers your email list adds over a given period of time. This metric also measures the success of additional marketing campaigns your organization is running to increase recipients. This is a great metric for tying marketing strategies together.

- **Conversion Rates** are the percentage of recipients who engaged in your campaign's desired action and outcome (e.g., signed up for an opportunity). This is arguably the most important metric for judging the success of your email marketing efforts. However, keep in mind that the other KPIs mentioned above will have an impact on your organization's ability to reach high conversion rates, so it's not wise to focus solely on one KPI above all others.

DIGITAL CONTENT MARKETING KPI'S

Digital content marketing is a strategy that has been proven to work effectively for nonprofit organizations due, in part, to the power of storytelling. A recent study actually found that 78% of prospects prefer learning about an organization via articles rather than ads.[61] The old saying "content is king" is still relevant as of the publication of this book. Creating and driving results from content requires careful planning and execution. The importance of having an end goal in mind when creating strategic content for your nonprofit can't be stressed enough. Content marketing is a little different than other channels in that your organization should group content pieces by funnel placement. In other words, content should fall into either top, middle or bottom of the funnel based on your campaign goals. Here are KPI's to measure your online content strategy:

- **Organic Users on Website** (Filtered by Pageviews): Content today should be written with SEO in mind. Your nonprofits content should be planned with the goal of reaching audiences based on their search behavior. Seeing high organic entrances and pageviews on a specific content piece means that your content is doing well in search. Please note that just because your content is attracting visits does not necessarily mean its targeting the right audience. We will cover those KPI's below.

- **Content Click-through Rates** (Filtered by Page): Similar to the email KPI above content click-through rates can help your organization to determine the overall engagement level with your content campaigns and provide insights into which individual pieces resonated the most with your target audience. If your audience is clicking around the information is relevant to them.

- **New vs Returning Visitors** (Filtered by Page): Benchmarking new vs returning visitors to each of your unique content pieces can provide visibility into its reach and engagement level. If visitors are returning it means that the content is worthy of multiple looks and consideration. If the piece is driving new users that are digesting the content and engaging with it (remember CTR) then you may want to create additional content pieces on the same topic.

- **Conversion Rates** (Goals): Conversion rates should be a key metric of success. Conversion rates may not necessarily mean lead generation. Your organization will need to develop a plan for what you want each content piece to achieve. Setting up a system for measuring conversion rates will allow you and your team to see if each piece is meeting its goal. As mentioned earlier the goal of some content pieces may be to move traffic to other pieces that are lower in the conversion funnel.

SOCIAL MEDIA MARKETING KPI'S

Social media is one marketing channel for which people have a hard time measuring KPIs and justifying the investment. The good news is that, like any other channel, success on social media can be measured by tracking a few key metrics. Again, the metrics that your organization measures and reports on depend on your overall goal for social media and the channel being analyzed for success. Here are a few common social media KPIs you might apply to your marketing efforts:

- **Clicks and Conversions**: Many organizations use social sharing as a means to drive traffic to website calls to action. This is a good strategy for increasing a nonprofit's website visibility. Use tools like Google Analytics to determine how much traffic is entering your organization's site from social media and how many of those visitors are completing the desired action. In addition, be sure to measure this activity against your set goal.
- **Likes** (Engagement): Getting social media likes is a good indication that your audience is engaging with and consuming your content. Review your posts and keep track of which content is getting the most likes from your audience. Once you identify a pattern, you can create additional content pieces to share based on your most engaging topics.
- **Shares** (Engagement): Another engagement metric to measure is the number of shares your content is receiving. Shares are another indication that your audience is resonating with the content your organization is posting. Keep track of which content pieces are being shared the most and look for trends in either the content or the post itself.

- **Followers and Fans:** One of the biggest benefits of social media for nonprofits is the ability to build a community and reach large numbers of people. Tracking how many followers you have and attract each month is a good indication of social growth. Measuring followers can also help your organization forecast future social growth and how many volunteers and prospects can be engaged.

Reporting and measuring marketing KPIs will help your nonprofit better understand what channels are reaching volunteer prospects and driving conversions and engagement. However, marketing is yet another component of your overall volunteer program that can be optimized via a data-driven decision-making process. If your organization is not making volunteer management decisions based on real and measurable data, your program is missing out on opportunities for growth.

Simply tracking your marketing initiatives are only a part of a much bigger picture. Becoming a data-driven organization in not just one but a number of strategic areas can set your organization up for success in meeting its overall volunteer program objectives. It's simply a matter of understanding which types of data are important and developing strategies to apply that data to your volunteer program in a meaningful way.

ENHANCING VOLUNTEER MANAGEMENT BY BECOMING DATA-DRIVEN

"Because the people who are crazy enough to think they can change the world are the ones who do."

– Steve Jobs

Measuring and recording marketing metrics is just one step that your organization can take to become data-driven. Becoming data-driven is an organization-wide decision to enhance insights, create positioning, and optimize operations. In fact, all nonprofit departments can reap the rewards of capturing, analyzing, and making strategy decisions based on real data.

Keep in mind that the data your organization collects should only be data that will have an impact on the way that your nonprofit acts and positions itself in the future. Collecting too much data and not making adjustments based on results can actually cause more harm than good, so you'll need to be sure the data points your nonprofit focuses on are specific and actionable.

There are four types of data most nonprofits find value in tracking.

- **Qualitative Data:** Information that can't actually be measured through traditional means is considered qualitative. This form of data is not numerical and can include a large number of variables and information. Nonprofits can capture qualitative data from a variety of sources, including case notes, verbal reports, surveys, and feedback from volunteers and staff. Measuring qualitative data is essential, since valuable information gathered can often be missed when only capturing quantitative data. Qualitative data can help fill in the gaps and create a full story around fact-based information.

- **Failure Data:** Often times it takes a lot of failures to reach success. Keeping track of which strategies did not work, why they didn't work, and what your organization is doing to change direction is just as important as reporting positive results. The key to identifying actionable failure data is to set your campaign goals ahead of time, stick to a written plan, and discard assumptions. Data measurement should only be based on facts (both good and bad). Understanding your volunteer management failures is one of the best ways to improve your processes and better engage constituents in the future.

- **Mission Impact Data:** This data justifies or exposes opportunities for your organization to fulfil its promise to the community. Mission impact data is one of the most important sets of metrics to measure, as it can provide valuable insights into how the community, volunteers, and other stakeholders view your nonprofit's progress and whether or not your organization is hitting its goal of mission attainment.

- **Volunteer Impact Data:** Demonstrating the successes, failures, opportunities, and weaknesses of your organization's volunteer program and whether volunteerism is contributing to mission attainment should be a crucial component of optimizing your organization's volunteer management strategy. In fact, measuring and acting on volunteer impact data can help streamline the management process as a whole.

FOCUSING ON ACTIONABLE METRICS

Measuring the success of your volunteer management process and program begins with identifying actionable metrics. Setting SMART goals ensures that your volunteer program's objectives are specific, measurable, achievable, relevant and time-bound. Once your organization has set volunteer program goals it becomes much easier to determine a strategy for measuring success and optimizing efforts with metrics.

Your goals will vary based on your organization's current objectives. Below are a few examples of common goals and supporting metrics used by nonprofits aiming to improve their volunteer management strategies.

GOAL: INCREASE VOLUNTEER RETENTION RATES	
METRIC (QUANTITATIVE)	**EXAMPLE**
(returning volunteers) ÷ (total volunteers) = retention rate	After launching a gamification campaign in Q3, a nonprofit found that 702 of its total 1,206 volunteers returned, yielding a retention rate of **58%**.

GOAL: IDENTIFY GAPS IN VOLUNTEER SATISFACTION	
METRIC (QUALITATIVE)	**EXAMPLE**
Solicit direct feedback from volunteers	A nonprofit launches a satisfaction survey annually, then reviews the survey feedback and identifies response patterns. Results indicate **40%** of respondents mention **training** as a program area that needs improvement.

GOAL: INCREASE RECRUITMENT AND ANNUAL VOLUNTEER TIME VALUE	
METRIC (QUANTITATIVE)	**EXAMPLE**
annual volunteer hours x value of volunteer hour = **annual value**	A nonprofit launches a new volunteer management solution at the end of 2016. After determining the value of a volunteer hour to be worth $23.33 in their state, they multiply that value by their volunteers' 10,000 total hours for 2017 to find an annual value of **$233,300**, an **increase** over the previous year's annual value of $168,033.

BEING TRANSPARENT & ACCESSIBLE

It is crucial that your organization is transparent and accessible both in collecting data for analysis and in sharing information with shareholders, such as staff, volunteers, and investors. Being transparent and accessible should apply to all of your organization's data- collection methods, types of data, and collection results. Being transparent and accessible is a great way to let shareholders know what your nonprofit is monitoring and what adjustments and initiatives are being considered to improve results in the future. Providing shareholders with data also helps reinforce their commitment to your cause, both from a time and financial investment perspective.

Here are a few ways to be transparent and accessible with data and data -collection practices:

- Provide current volunteer program metrics to all organizational departments so they understand why you plan on deploying specific improvement initiatives in the future.
- Let investors know what their money will be used for and why based on metrics captured.
- Explain the purpose of surveys and other data collection practices to volunteers in order to yield honest responses and productive feedback.
- Provide cause, fundraising, and volunteer program data to shareholders on a regular basis.

USING DATA TO MEASURE VOLUNTEER IMPACT

According to a 2014 study performed by Software Advice, only 55% of nonprofits assess volunteer impact and use that impact data to define and optimize their volunteer strategy[62]. As the importance and value of volunteers continues to increase year over year, so does the importance of measuring their impact to improve decision-making processes and program direction. Routinely measuring volunteer impact and planning strategies based on results will help your nonprofit move the needle on retention, engagement, satisfaction, and volunteer value.

Volunteer impact metrics can help your nonprofit measure:

- **Volunteer Satisfaction and Engagement:** Organizations can measure program satisfaction by creating, sending and analyzing the results of a volunteer satisfaction survey. Each volunteer fulfilling an opportunity should be sent a survey as a follow-up. It is key that organizations make surveying a part of their processes to capture the best actionable data from supporters.
- **New vs. Repeat Volunteers:** Knowing who your volunteers are and where they came from is essential. Measuring new volunteers against repeat volunteers can help your nonprofit determine what source best drives volunteers to action, what the program's retention rate is, and how often its supporters provide their time. Nonprofits can most easily measure this metric by using volunteer management software.
- **Volunteer Attendance:** Analyzing volunteer attendance is often overlooked as a KPI. Nonprofits that identify trends in their volunteer attendance rate may be able to pinpoint and address the problem areas causing no-shows. Volunteer attendance is another metric that good volunteer software can provide quickly.
- **Volunteer Footprint:** Another important metric to understand is how many organizational roles are fulfilled by volunteers. Many nonprofits use volunteers in almost all departments. There are also nonprofits that are fully staffed by volunteers. Identifying volunteer footprint can help a nonprofit estimate the total dollar value of time donated.
- **Opportunity Costs:** It is key that nonprofits measure the cost of a volunteer hour. Organizations should consider costs for training, rewards, and development, as well as any other costs that go into their volunteer program.

- **Social Media Shares**: Social media is a great way for nonprofits to share volunteer opportunities with the community. Measuring social shares can help an organization identify how people are responding to their program online.
- **Volunteer vs. Non-Volunteer Donations**: Many organizations report that their volunteers are also some of their biggest financial donors. Research   shows that two-thirds of volunteers donate money to the same organization they donate their time to.[63] Measuring this key relationship can help organizations add additional value to their volunteer program and enhance their understanding of key supporters.

Real data is helping nonprofits understand the value of their volunteers, discover opportunities to streamline their processes, and create strategies that address weak points in their volunteer programs. Deploying a volunteer management solution can significantly improve your organization's potential to capture, analyze and create volunteer impact reporting to share with stakeholders.

COMMUNICATING WITH VOLUNTEERS EFFECTIVELY

"The most important thing in communication is hearing what isn't said."

– Peter Drucker

P roper use of communication strategy allows your organization to engage volunteers, introduce them to new opportunities, and leverage your data collected to increase retention rates. Good communication may seem like an obvious engagement tactic but you would be surprised to know that many organizations struggle to communicate with volunteers effectively. A study by Nonprofit Marketing Guide found that participating nonprofits ranked their communication effectiveness at only 3.3 out of 5 stars.[64] In today's highly competitive nonprofit space, a 66% communication effectiveness score won't cut it if you hope to engage volunteers enough to retain them and covert them to lifelong supporters.

Let's take a look at a variety of strategies your nonprofit can utilize in order to communicate more effectively with your volunteers and shareholders.

COMMUNICATE EARLY AND OFTEN

As discussed previously, volunteer motivations and activity have changed over the years, as has the many ways technology can assist in managing them. Communication is no different. Today's volunteers want to hear from your organization early and often. Online tools provide feature sets to make it possible to communicate both quickly and strategically with your volunteers.

Did you know that 44% of participants in a recent study said that they volunteered because they were asked to do so?[65] Keeping in mind that the value of a volunteer hour is typically over $24.00, that means that each missed recruitment opportunity due to failure to communicate can cost your nonprofit big money over time. Communicating early and often can ensure your supporters have complete visibility into your organization's ongoing needs. Having access to an automated volunteer management platform can turn capturing volunteer data and communicating quickly into a streamlined and measurable process. Volunteer management platforms like VolunteerHub allow nonprofits to organize their volunteer database, set up automated email and mobile notifications, send targeted email campaigns and track volunteer communication engagement over time.

How soon and often you communicate with volunteers comes down to the preferences of your volunteer base as well as your organization's communication capabilities and limitations (e.g., lack of staff, time, or the proper tools). Best practices suggest that your organization communicate with volunteers as soon as they show interest in your opportunities. Once a prospective volunteer is in your database, it is essential that you communicate with them from start to finish over the lifetime of their service.

Many nonprofits find that engaging their volunteer base through ongoing communications increases their retention rate and alleviates some recruitment pressure. Communication can — and should — be used frequently to inform supporters of new opportunities, organizational changes, mission attainment, and appreciation. Your nonprofit should also communicate with volunteers frequently in order to identify strengths, weaknesses, challenges, and program desires. Long-term, regular communication offers your organization an opportunity to build a bond with each supporter and strengthen your volunteer program as a whole.

COMMUNICATE ACROSS SEVERAL CHANNELS

One of the keys to communication with volunteers is delivering messages across multiple channels. When developing a communication strategy, consider the demographic of your volunteer base and ask them for their preferred communication method. Surveying volunteers and identifying best communication channels will ensure that supporters are receiving your organization's updates and opportunity outreach messaging. Remember when developing a communication strategy to use your organization's data and current supporters' preferences to dictate the direction of the most optimal channels to reach your audience.

In 2016, the Nonprofit Marketing Guide conducted a survey of 1,600 nonprofit professionals to identify the top communication channels in the nonprofit space for communicating with volunteers:[66]

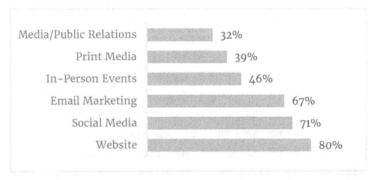

Media/Public Relations	32%
Print Media	39%
In-Person Events	46%
Email Marketing	67%
Social Media	71%
Website	80%

Notice that the data above emphasize the importance of investing in a web-based tool, such as volunteer management solution, that communicates opportunities for involvement frequently and effectively. The data also demonstrates how communicating digitally is becoming the most effective communication avenue in the nonprofit industry. The importance of online communication shouldn't be a surprise, however, as 84% of U.S. households own and use a computer on a daily basis.[67]

CREATE A TARGETED COMMUNICATION PLAN FOR EACH SEGMENT

Understanding your volunteer base can help your organization create a plan for communicating and engaging with each volunteer type that your organization recruits. Communicating effectively with volunteers therefore involves creating segments (groups of volunteers that share similarities) for each of your volunteer demographics. Researching these similarities and documenting them can create more successful communication techniques. For example, how you communicate with millennial volunteers may differ substantially from how you communicate with senior volunteers. Therefore, the best way to create a strategy for communicating with each segment is to ask supporters for their preferred communication channel and capture demographical information about each volunteer.

Having access to a centralized volunteer database in conjunction with a CRM system can make the process of creating segments and organizing them much easier for your nonprofit. Using a volunteer database and CRM to organize segments can also help ensure that volunteers are not missed, communication is fast and efficient, and messaging is direct and relevant to each targeted group. Finally, access to a volunteer database and CRM system reduces the amount of data entry and organization time for your nonprofit's staff. Saved time can be used to get to know volunteers better, allowing you to create personalized messaging and focus on other areas of your volunteer program that need improvement.

Here are a few strategic tips for communicating by segment:

- Accept and understand that not all volunteers are the same.
- Get to know each of your volunteer segments and their communication styles well.

- Develop and deploy communication activities and strategies based on the information you know about each segment.
- Focus communications around the "wants" of each segment.
- Adjust the frequency of communications around the engagement level of campaigns. However, be careful not to over-communicate, as that can actually decrease engagement over time.

USE COMMUNICATION TO VOICE APPRECIATION

It's no secret that volunteers want to feel appreciated in exchange for their commitment to your cause. Feeling appreciated and being thanked regularly is one of the top reasons volunteers continue to provide their valuable time. Remember, your nonprofit organization could not achieve its goals without volunteerism, so using communication in your strategy for showing appreciation is essential to create engagement and increase retention.

Appreciation is on the mind of many business leaders. In a study completed in 2018, 58% of volunteers said that appreciation has the biggest impact on their ability to engage.[68] The same study also reported that organizations with an effective recognition program have 31% lower turnover rates than organizations with ineffective strategies. These statistics clearly demonstrate the importance of strategic recognition.

Here are a few tips for communicating appreciation to your volunteers:

- Make appreciation a top priority in your communication strategy.
- Be sincere.
- Thank volunteers often and in a variety of ways.
- Share community impact.
- Communicate consistently and on a timely basis.
- Personalize the experience.

- Don't forget that hand-written thank you notes are still a valuable means of showing appreciation.

Communicating appreciation to volunteers is much easier and can be more cost-effective than you may think. There are many ways to communicate with volunteers and thank them for opportunity fulfilment; for instance, a volunteer management tool can provide options for both customized and automated appreciation messages. However, don't forget that how you communicate appreciation still depends on your organization's volunteer segments and communication channels.

THE FUTURE OF VOLUNTEERISM AND VOLUNTEER MANAGEMENT

"The best way to predict your future is to create it."

– Abraham Lincoln

Volunteerism and how nonprofits manage their volunteers effectively has changed substantially over the years. Today's volunteers are looking to make a difference and to be engaged at the same time. The value of a volunteer hour is a factor that both nonprofits and volunteers are beginning to realize, and the importance of deploying strategies to keep volunteers interacting with your nonprofit's brand continues to grow in importance.

Previous chapters of this book touched on the importance of engaging, retaining, and providing value to volunteers in exchange for their time. However, understanding the history of volunteerism and what it means to volunteer today is just the beginning. It's also important to stay ahead of trends by looking into future of volunteerism and where volunteer management appears to be heading.

Just as volunteerism has changed dramatically since it's inception, opportunity fulfilment trends continue to evolve, technology continues to be adapted to changing needs, and new and future means of engaging volunteers continue to be developed. Staying ahead of the curve can help your organization remain current on volunteerism trends and engagement initiatives.

THE FUTURE OF OPPORTUNITY FULFILLMENT

Opportunity fulfilment is likely the one aspect of volunteerism that has changed the most compared to previous generations. In the early days of volunteerism, supporters registered and provided their service locally, face-to-face with the coordinator. Today, technology is allowing volunteers to find and fill opportunities whenever and wherever they are. Organizations that use a volunteer management system are able to create opportunities, share them on their website, and allow volunteers to register quickly and efficiently. Volunteer management tools are also making the process of organizing data, communicating with supporters, and creating program reports much easier for nonprofit organizations.

The use of technology to allow supporters to self-register for volunteer opportunities is quickly becoming the market standard for nonprofits to enhance their recruitment process. In fact, 67% of people who volunteered in 2016 found their opportunity online, up almost 100% compared with 34% just ten years prior.[69] An online registration process benefits both nonprofits and the volunteers who provide service, and new volunteer management software features will continue to become available over time to appeal to volunteers and make tracking data easier for organizations.

The future also holds greater adaption of online recruitment tools by the senior generation. Seniors are learning technologies and accepting them into their daily routines at a rapid rate! A study by Braun Research found that over half of those volunteers aged 65 and older are comfortable using technology, and this number is climbing steadily each year. The ability to use volunteer management tools to recruit more senior volunteers is big news for the health of the nonprofit industry and the communities that they serve. Just in 2017 alone, 20.7 million older adults contributed more than 3.3 billion hours of service in 2017 alone, equating to a value of more than $75 billion.[70] Knowing this, the fear of using technology to reach senior volunteer prospects is diminishing every day.

In addition to streamlining volunteer management through online solutions, there are several ways that opportunity fulfilment has changed and several trends that we will continue to see in the future. Remote opportunity fulfilment, for instance, is also growing in popularity. Many nonprofits are looking for remote talent to fill business function roles. Opening up recruitment to remote volunteers is therefore increasing the number of opportunity prospects and the available talent pool. As technology continues to advance, chances are we will continue to see more remote opportunities and new ways to manage remote volunteers advance.

Another opportunity fulfilment trend that has and will continue to grow in popularity is the appearance of volunteer abroad programs and volunteer vacations, commonly referred to as "voluntourism." The goal of these programs is to provide purpose and enrichment to a potential supporter's travels. Voluntourism offers volunteers the opportunity to experience new locations and cultures while committing their time to the greater good, while also benefiting volunteer organizations. These programs offer nonprofits another strategic way to increase their prospect talent pool and create differentiators for their volunteer programs. In addition, voluntourism is a strategy that will continue to appeal to millennials in the future; 84% of surveyed millennials said they would travel abroad to participate in volunteer activities, and it is anticipated that voluntourism and international volunteering will continue to evolve in the future and become a widely accepted strategy for nonprofits to stand out to prospects.[71]

Finally, technology is being used every day to enhance volunteer experiences, make fulfilment fun, and reward supporters for their service. Nonprofits have begun to identify and deploy unique ways of adding value to the lives of their volunteers. In addition to providing supporters with personal benefits like professional development, skill attainment, social benefits, and more, nonprofits are increasingly using these incentives in conjunction with the ultimate benefit that volunteerism provides: an ability to help the community. However, as the nonprofit space becomes more competitive, the need for additional benefits to recruit volunteers becomes greater.

As discussed previously, providing recognition to volunteers is key. Gamification — the application of gaming elements such as competition and rewards into everyday tasks — is a growing strategy in the nonprofit space and is a simple way to engage, recognize and reward volunteers. Gamification involves setting a goal for supporters, tracking their progress, and providing them with rewards for their service. The adoption and application of a recognition and rewards program is likely to advance significantly in the next few years as nonprofits continue their efforts to strengthen their volunteer and fundraising programs. In addition, leading volunteer management solutions like VolunteerHub are beginning to offer gamification as a feature to keep up with these trends as gamification becomes a go-to strategy for engaging supporters in the years to come.

MAKING A BIGGER IMPACT

As technology advances, so too does the ability for nonprofits to make a bigger impact in the communities they serve. New technologies are being created every year to help organizations manage volunteers, broadcast opportunities, and increase their reach. Technology is also making it possible for organizations to allocate time towards the development of strategic partnerships both internally and externally. Furthermore, a growing shift in the nonprofit space creates a larger and larger impact on volunteer trends as more for-profit organizations become involved with volunteer organizations through corporate partnerships and resource allocation. And volunteerism continues to evolve.

Volunteerism and the nonprofit industry as a whole have come a long way since Benjamin Franklin founded that first volunteer-run firehouse, but the premise for volunteerism remains the same: As long as there are problems in the world, communities will continue to need volunteers to help solve them. Nonprofits will be seen as a source of innovation in pursuit of solving social issues with focus and determination. Volunteering is — and will continue to be — one of the most important actions we can take to secure a greater future for our communities and our world.

We are proud to be a part of it.

NOTES

[1] Jennie Cohen, "Roster From Ben Franklin's Fire Department Found," History.com, May 23, 2012, https://www.history.com/news/roster-from-ben-franklins-fire-department-found.

[2] "In Case of Fire," USHistory.org, accessed June 12, 2018, http://www.ushistory.org/franklin/philadelphia/fire.htm.

[3] Merritt Long, "History of Volunteer Firefighting," My Figrefighter Nation, August 12, 2007, https://my.firefighternation.com/forum/topics/889755:Topic:23687?groupUrl=firefightinghistorymyths.

[4] Hylton J. G. Haynes and Gary P. Stein, "U.S. fire department profile," National Fire Protection Association, April 1, 2017, https://www.nfpa.org/News-and-Research/Fire-statistics-and-reports/Fire-statistics/The-fire-service/Administration/US-fire-department-profile.

[5] Christine Leigh Heyrman, "The First Great Awakening," *Divining America*, *TeacherServe©*, National Humanities Center, accessed April 25, 2018, http://nationalhumanitiescenter.org/tserve/eighteen/ekeyinfo/grawaken.htm.

[6] YMCA of the USA, "Organizational Profile," accessed June 12, 2018, http://www.ymca.net/organizational-profile.

[7] "Our History," American Red Cross, accessed June 12, 2018, http://www.redcross.org/about-us/who-we-are/history.

[8] "United Way Celebrates 125 Years! - A little history...," Greater Gallatin United Way, accessed June 12, 2018,

https://www.greatergallatinunitedway.org/news/united-way-celebrates-125-years-little-history.

⁹ "Wilson asks for declaration of war," *This Day in History*, History TV, accessed June 8, 2018, https://www.history.com/this-day-in-history/wilson-asks-for-declaration-of-war.

¹⁰ "Volunteers during the First World War," British Red Cross, accessed February 6, 2018, https://vad.redcross.org.uk/Volunteers-during-WW1.

¹¹ Carol Harris, "1914-1918: How charities helped to win WW1," Third Sector, June 27, 2014, https://www.thirdsector.co.uk/1914-1918-charities-helped-win-ww1/volunteering/article/1299786.

¹² "Volunteers during the First World War."

¹³ "Great Depression," History.com, accessed March 1, 2018, https://www.history.com/topics/great-depression.

¹⁴ "World War 2 Statistics," Second World War History, accessed June 12, 2018, https://www.secondworldwarhistory.com/world-war-2-statistics.asp.

¹⁵ "The Charitable Sector," Independent Sector, accessed February 7, 2018, https://independentsector.org/about/the-charitable-sector.

¹⁶ Elizabeth T. Boris, Erwin de Leon, Katie L. Roeger, and Milena Nikolova, "Human Service Nonprofits and Government Collaboration," National Council of Nonprofits, October 1, 2010, https://www.councilofnonprofits.org/sites/default/files/documents/Full%20Report.pdf.

¹⁷ "Massive earthquake strikes Haiti," *This Day in History*, History.com, accessed July 3, 2018, https://www.history.com/this-day-in-history/massive-earthquake-strikes-haiti.

¹⁸ Becky Oskin, "Japan Earthquake & Tsunami of 2011: Facts and Information," Live Science, September 18, 2017, https://www.livescience.com/39110-japan-2011-earthquake-tsunami-facts.html.

¹⁹ Frank Barry, "One Thing Most Nonprofits Stink at (Donor Retention) and How You Can Change It in 2017," npENGAGE (blog), February 26, 2017, https://npengage.com/nonprofit-fundraising/12-donor-retention-tips-from-nonprofit-fundraising-experts/ [Accessed 12 Jun. 2018].

[20] Steve MacLaughlin, "2016 Charitable Giving Report," Blackbaud Institute, February 1, 2017, https://institute.blackbaud.com/asset/2016-charitable-giving-report.

[21] Marshall Goldsmith, "4 Tips for Efficient Succession Planning," Harvard Business Review, May 12, 2009, https://hbr.org/2009/05/change-succession-planning-to.

[22] Yvonne Siu, "Skills-Based Volunteering for Small Businesses: Getting Started," A Billion + Change, April 10, 2013, http://www.pointsoflight.org/sites/default/files/resources/files/skills-based_volunteering_for_smes.pdf.

[23] "The Charitable Sector."

[24] "Volunteering in the United States, 2015," United States Department of Labor, February 25, 2016, https://www.bls.gov/news.release/volun.nr0.htm.

[25] "Do Companies Really Care About Volunteer Experiences?," Uduni, February 7, 2016, http://uduni.com/career-tips/do-companies-really-care-about-volunteer-experiences.

[26] "Doing Good is Good for You: 2013 Health and Volunteering Study," UnitedHealth Group, June 18, 2013, http://www.unitedhealthgroup.com/~/media/UHG/PDF/2013/UNH-Health-Volunteering-Study.ashx.

[27] "Doing Good is Good for You: 2013 Health and Volunteering Study."

[28] "Economic Impact," National Council of Nonprofits, accessed June 13, 2018, https://www.councilofnonprofits.org/economic-impact.

[29] "2012: The Year of Friends with Benefits," The DoSomething.org Index on Young People and Volunteering, accessed June 13, 2018, https://www.dosomething.org/sites/default/files/blog/2012-Web-Singleview_0.pdf.

[30] Carmen Perez, "Pro Bono Service: Not Just For Lawyers Anymore!," HuffPost (blog), last modified December 6, 2017, https://www.huffingtonpost.com/carmen-perez/pro-bono-service-not-just_b_12574804.html.

[31] Jeff Jowdy, "4 Ways to Turn Volunteers Into Donors," NonProfit PRO, February 13, 2013, https://www.nonprofitpro.com/article/4-ways-turn-volunteers-into-donors/all.

[32] "Overcoming Barriers to Giving," Fidelity Charitable, November 17, 2017, https://www.fidelitycharitable.org/docs/overcoming-barriers-to-giving.pdf.

[33] "Overcoming Barriers to Giving."

[34] "State Rankings by Volunteer Retention Rate," Corporation for National and Community Service, accessed June 1, 2018, https://www.nationalservice.gov/vcla/state-rankings-volunteer-retention-rate.

[35] "Volunteering in the United States, 2015."

[36] Karl Zinsmeister, "Statistics on U.S. Generosity," *The Almanac of American Philanthropy: 2017 Compact Edition* (Washington D.C.: Philanthropy Roundtable, 2017), 342-343.

[37] Melissa McGlensey, "64% Of Donations Are Made By Women.. And Other Facts About How We Give," HuffPost (blog), last modified December 6, 2017, https://www.huffingtonpost.com/2014/04/29/infographic-shows-charity-is-more-than-money_n_5233390.html.

[38] Karl Zinsmeister, "Who Gives Most to Charity," Philanthropy Roundtable, accessed July 3, 2018, https://www.philanthropyroundtable.org/almanac/statistics/who-gives.

[39] Justin McGill, "How to Develop a Content Strategy: A Start-to-Finish Guide," Hubspot (blog), last modified May 16, 2018, https://blog.hubspot.com/marketing/content-marketing-plan.

[40] "Nonprofit Marketing Statistics That Matter," Ironpaper, February 21, 2015, http://www.ironpaper.com/webintel/articles/nonprofit-marketing-statistics-for-2015.

[41] "Average Open Rate for Email & Other Email Benchmarks," MailChimp, accessed June 9, 2018, https://mailchimp.com/resources/research/email-marketing-benchmarks.

[42] Steve MacLaughlin, "50 Fascinating Nonprofit Statistics," npENGAGE, October 17, 2016, https://npengage.com/nonprofit-news/50-fascinating-nonprofit-statistics.

[43] Michal Leszczynski, "The State Of Email Marketing By Industry, GetResponse (blog), February 15, 2016, https://blog.getresponse.com/the-state-of-email-marketing-by-industry.html.

[44] Lindsay Kolowich, "Email Analytics: The 6 Email Marketing Metrics & KPIs You Should Be Tracking," Hubspot (blog), last modified January 3, 2018,

https://blog.hubspot.com/marketing/metrics-email-marketers-should-be-tracking.

[45] "Average Open Rate for Email & Other Email Benchmarks."

[46] Kim Stiglitz, "70 Email Marketing Stats You Need to Know," Campaignmonitor.com (blog), January 6, 2016, https://www.campaignmonitor.com/blog/email-marketing/2016/01/70-email-marketing-stats-you-need-to-know.

[47] "Nonprofit Marketing Statistics That Matter."

[48] Jason Firch, "39 Nonprofit Content Marketing Trends You Need To Know," Nonprofits Source, last modified March 21, 2018, https://nonprofitssource.com/nonprofit-content-marketing-trends-you-need-to-know-infographic.

[49] Julia McCoy, "9 Stats That Will Make You Want to Invest in Content Marketing," Content Marketing Institute, October 22, 2017, https://contentmarketinginstitute.com/2017/10/stats-invest-content-marketing.

[50] Julia McCoy, "9 Stats That Will Make You Want to Invest in Content Marketing."

[51] "For Driving Engagement, B2B Marketers Put a Premium on Content," eMarketer, April 8, 2018, https://www.emarketer.com/Article/Driving-Engagement-B2B-Marketers-Put-Premium-on-Content/1009790.

[52] Julia McCoy, "9 Stats That Will Make You Want to Invest in Content Marketing."

[53] Steve Olenski, "The Ups and Downs of B2B Content Marketing," *Forbes* online, Ocotber 11, 2016, https://www.forbes.com/sites/steveolenski/2016/10/11/the-ups-and-downs-of-b2b-content-marketing/#e97a0be60232.

[54] "Nonprofit Marketing Statistics That Matter."

[55] "The Millennial Impact Report: 2012," The Case Foundation, June 8, 2012, https://casefoundation.org/wp-content/uploads/2014/11/MillennialImpactReport-2012.pdf.

[56] "10 Technology Adoption And Success Stats From Nonprofits," TechImpact (blog), accessed July 3, 2018, http://blog.techimpact.org/10-nonprofit-tech-stats-on-digital-planning.

[57] Mary Lister, "40 Essential Social Media Marketing Statistics for 2018," WordStream (blog), July 25, 2018,

https://www.wordstream.com/blog/ws/2017/01/05/social-media-marketing-statistics.

58 "Content Marketing Infographic," Demand Metric, accessed March 10, 2018, https://www.demandmetric.com/content/content-marketing-infographic.

59 Olivia Allen, "How to Write Catchy Email Subject Lines: 19 Tips," Hubspot (blog), last modified July 30, 2018, https://blog.hubspot.com/marketing/improve-your-email-subject-line.

60 Tony Glowacki et al., "Fundraising's Social Revolution," Wealth Engine, January 8, 2013, https://www.wealthengine.com/sites/default/files/imce/Fundraising_Social_Revolution_NP.pdf.

61 Tom Pick, "104 Fascinating Social Media and Marketing Statistics for 2014 (and 2015)," Business 2 Community, December 2, 2014, https://www.business2community.com/social-media/104-fascinating-social-media-marketing-statistics-2014-2015-01084935.

62 Janna Finch, "Volunteer Impact Report: IndustryView 2014," Software Advice, September 22, 2014, https://www.softwareadvice.com/nonprofit/industryview/volunteer-impact-report-2014.

63 "Time and Money: The Role of Volunteering in Philanthropy," Fidelity Charitable, January 26, 2015, https://www.fidelitycharitable.org/docs/volunteering-and-philanthropy.pdf.

64 Kivi Leroux Miller, "2017 Nonprofit Communications Trends Report," Nonprofit Marketing Guide, January 29, 2017, http://nonprofitmarketingguide.com/freemembers/2017NonprofitCommunicationsTrendsReport.pdf.

65 Norah McClintock, "Understanding Canadian Volunteers," Imagine Canada, June 13, 2011, http://www.imaginecanada.ca/sites/default/files/www/en/giving/reports/understanding_volunteers.pdf.

66 Kivi Leroux Miller, "2017 Nonprofit Communications Trends Report."

[67] Thom File and Camille Ryan, "Computer and Internet Use in the United States: 2013," November 17, 2014, https://www.census.gov/history/pdf/acs-internet2013.pdf.

[68] Dave Anderson, "How Nonprofit Organizations (NPOs) Can Hire Great Employees," RecuirterBox (blog), accessed August 1, 2018, https://recruiterbox.com/blog/how-nonprofits-npos-can-hire-great-employees.

[69] Amanda Khozi Mukwashi et al., "2015 State of the World's Volunteerism Report," United Nations Volunteers, May 21, 2015, https://www.unv.org/sites/default/files/2015%20State%20of%20the%20World%27s%20Volunteerism%20Report%20-%20Transforming%20Governance.pdf.

[70] Bethany Stoutamire and Leacey E. Brown, "Volunteering: More than an act of service, iGrow, September 11, 2017, http://igrow.org/healthy-families/aging/volunteering-more-than-an-act-of-service.

[71] Rebecca Dalzell, "The Young and the Charitable: Millennials Make More of Travel Experiences," JPMorgan Chase and Co., last modified November 10, 2017, https://www.chase.com/news/072415-millenials-travel-experiences.

CPSIA information can be obtained
at www.ICGtesting.com
Printed in the USA
LVHW021249021222
734416LV00004B/746